Theorizing in Organization Studies

Theorizing in Organization Studies

Insights from Key Thinkers

Anne Vorre Hansen

Department of Social Sciences and Business, Roskilde University, Denmark

Sabine Madsen

Department of Politics and Society, Aalborg University, Denmark

Edward Elgar
PUBLISHING

Cheltenham, UK • Northampton, MA, USA

Cover image: drawing by Mary Jo Hatch given with kind permission, August 2018.

Published by
Edward Elgar Publishing Limited
The Lypiatts
15 Lansdown Road
Cheltenham
Glos GL50 2JA
UK

Edward Elgar Publishing, Inc.
William Pratt House
9 Dewey Court
Northampton
Massachusetts 01060
USA

Paperback edition 2020

A catalogue record for this book
is available from the British Library

Library of Congress Control Number: 2019935381

This book is available electronically in the **Elgar**online
Business subject collection
DOI 10.4337/9781788970044

ISBN 978 1 78897 003 7 (cased)
ISBN 978 1 78897 004 4 (eBook)
ISBN 978 1 80037 102 6 (paperback)

Typeset by Servis Filmsetting Ltd, Stockport, Cheshire
Printed and bound by CPI Group (UK) Ltd, Croydon, CR0 4YY

Contents

Boxes

Foreword

This book is short, fun to read, and full of good ideas. It also works well as an introduction to how to theorize in organization studies, for students as well as professors. The content is based on eight interviews with key figures in the field, reorganized by theme by the two authors who have also added comments of their own. The result makes for fresh and lively reading, reflecting the ambition of Anne Vorre Hansen and Sabine Madsen to say something new and to do so in a new way.

The topic of the book is theorizing and its main message is one of *inspiration*. The authors also want to present the reader with knowledge on the basics of theorizing, and they do a good job in this as well. First, however, they want to get the reader to theorize herself or himself.

Theorizing is the process through which a theory is created, from the first feeble hunch to the final theory, presented in print to the reader. This whole process, the authors emphasize very strongly, is personal – it is *you* who theorize. You must not repeat or channel someone else's ideas. This would be to turn yourself into a ventriloquist's dummy! You must 'dare to find your own approach to theorizing, and as a very important point thereof – your own voice'.

It is also important to realize that it is not possible to theorize well in organizational studies just by sitting down at your computer and starting to create a theory. You first have to observe some phenomenon carefully; you also need to know quite a bit about your field. How to observe is something you learn in methods classes. How to develop ideas that resonate with your field, however, is more of a challenge. The authors' solution to this problem is that you first create a 'personal canon' of authors and books that are meaningful to you. They describe such a canon in the following way:

A close relationship with a few selected authors and their texts allows both for quick inspirational reading (because the thoughts are already familiar) and in-depth thinking and theorizing infused by the ideas and concepts of a small, consciously chosen family of thinkers. Thus, the building up of a personal canon seems to be a part of becoming yourself as an academic and of finding your own voice as a writer.

In addition to having a personal canon, it is also necessary to have a good knowledge of the literature in your field. To be able to draw on both these types of knowledge is a precondition for being creative in your theorizing. It also helps to know something about what is happening in fields other than your own:

In academia, the idiosyncratic is often frowned upon and considered a regrettable property of human cognition and behaviour. Here we suggest the opposite. Namely, that it is precisely due to close reading of a personal canon and a sense of belonging to (several) communities of thought – for example, philosophy, sociology, literary fiction – that are only vaguely or completely unrelated to the time and topics of one's field that it is possible to have ideas and develop theories that are new to the field.

Theorizing is also an activity that takes quite a bit of time, according to the authors. You may not want to follow a step-by-step procedure, they say, but you have to realize that what is involved is a process – and a process that takes time. You also have to get into the right kind of mood to theorize well. According to one of the authors:

For me, it is useful to think about the *process* of theorizing. When thinking about it as a process, it becomes more apparent and acceptable for me as a quite result-oriented person that it takes time, patience and effort to get to the results – and that the process is important and delightful in itself (at least some of it/to some extent). However, I think I would use the term 'to conceptualize' to express what it is I actually do during the process of theorizing. That is, during the process of theorizing I conceptualize the topic I am studying by experimenting with figures, tables, labels, names and metaphors to see if they fit. When the concepts seem to fit, it is (1) because they highlight the important differences and similarities (patterns) and foregrounds the unique aspects of (my own and/or others') experiences with the topic under study. And (2) because they make sense to others too, and not just to me.

In the last half of the quote, a mention is made of the centrality of concepts. This is a useful reminder of the fact that it is important to have a knowledge of concepts when you theorize, and know how to handle these when you are in the middle of an empirical analysis. To this can be added that just as there is a practical side to theorizing, there is also what may be called *a technical side*. By this last term I mean knowledge about what a concept is and what existing research about concepts can tell us. This also goes for other tools of the theorizer, such as analogy, abduction, visualization and more (see, e.g., Richard Swedberg, 2014a and 2016). Without a foundation of this type of knowledge it is difficult to theorize well. Social scientists have largely ignored this issue. This, however, is not the case in all of the sciences. Especially in philosophy and cognitive science there is abundant useful material of this type, which anyone interested in becoming good at theorizing will want to learn a bit about.

Some readers may want to know something about the position of this book by Anne Vorre Hansen and Sabine Madsen in the history of theorizing, especially in organization studies. First, there currently does not exist much material on theorizing in the social sciences. And much of what does exist is primarily on theory construction rather than on theorizing. These are closely related but theory construction is more formal in nature and close to the philosophy of science, while theorizing is much more realistic and practical in its approach (see, e.g., Shanyang Zhao, 1996). Another way to put it is that theory construction helps you to formulate the result of your theory work when it is ready for publication, and also to put it in such a form that it can be clearly understood and properly tested. Theorizing, in contrast, is more about dealing with the empirical problems you encounter on the way to the production of a full-fledged theory and also the difficulties you have to face in trying to explain a phenomenon. If the theorizer works a bit like a detective, and primarily wants to solve the case, the theory constructor takes over when the case is ready to enter the courthouse and has to be presented to the judge and jury. You always want to know who the culprit is (what the solution is), but you also need to prove the case according to the laws of the country (according to the norms of evidence in your field).

Even if the material on theorizing is small, there is more on this topic in organization studies than one might have thought. The reason for this may well be that this field from its inception and onwards has drawn on several disciplines; it has also continued to have one foot in academia and another in society at large. That there is a fair amount of material on theorizing in organization studies means that people from the other social sciences may want to know more about this and learn from it. For a very helpful introduction to the type of theorizing that works with models, there is first and foremost an excellent book by Charles Lave and James March: *An Introduction to Models in the Social Sciences* (1975). While this book is not focused on organization studies per se, quite a bit of the material is relevant for students of organization, such as the discussion of diffusion in Chapter 7. There are also several chapters that describe models from economics and psychology, and this material is easily applicable to organizations as well.

The intellectual core of the book by Charles Lave and James March, however, is to be found in its two introductory chapters devoted to the topic of speculation in theorizing. 'Speculation', according to Charles Lave and James March (1975, p. 2), 'is the soul of the social sciences'. It is especially useful to be good at speculation when you work on the explanation of some phenomenon. You need to learn to come up with many explanations, they argue; working with only one explanation is a mistake, in their view. Throughout their book the reader will also find a number of theoretical problems of the type that you encounter when you do empirical research, followed in bold letters by the words **STOP AND THINK**. The reason for this admonition is that students tend to read a book straight through, and not take time to stop and *think*. They are trained in how to read, but not to think. The two authors suggest a new version of Gresham's law (bad money drives out good): reading drives out thinking.

James March is not only known as a first-class student of organizations but also of many other topics and the same can be said of Arthur Stinchcombe, the author of another classical book on theorizing in social science. His book appeared in 1968 and is entitled *Constructing Social Theories*. While James March and Charles Lave are exclusively interested in models, Arthur Stinchcombe also discusses verbal theories. Both, however, are primarily interested in teaching students to theorize by coming up with many explanations.

Besides these two books, there are also a number of articles on theorizing in the literature on organizations. Some of the most important of these can be found in two theme issues on theory development that were published in *Academy of Management Review* in 1989 and 1999, and in an issue from 1995 of *Administrative Science Quarterly* that contains a discussion of 'what theory is' (Kimberly Elsbach, Robert Sutton and David Whetten, 1999; Robert Sutton and Barry Staw, 1995; David Whetten, 1989a). Many important issues are discussed in these articles, such as abstraction, imagination, and what differentiates theory from theorizing.

A special mention must also be made of the work on theorizing by Karl Weick because he is the person who has done the most during the last few decades to draw attention to the importance of theorizing in organization studies (see, e.g., Karl Weick, 1989, 1995, 2014). Karl Weick has summarized much of his work on theorizing in an article entitled 'The experience of theorizing', which is highly recommended (Karl Weick, 2005). Karl Weick's approach, like that of Anne Vorre Hansen and Sabine Madsen, is deeply personal in nature. It is not easy to summarize Weick's work in one sentence, but perhaps you can say that in his view it is by going back and forth between thinking and action that you are able to theorize and also to make sense of things. This goes for the analyst as well as people in general (everyone theorizes, in Karl Weick's view). For the analyst, including Karl Weick himself, writing is an especially important technique for theorizing.

During the last ten or so years, Weick has become something of a lone voice who advocates theorizing in organization studies. This book by Anne Vorre Hansen and Sabine Madsen is therefore extra welcome. This is also a good place to mention another of their many interesting ideas – that a book on theorizing does not come to an end once it has been finished and published. From this point on, they say, it is up to the reader to make it come alive, by allowing himself or herself to be inspired to start theorizing.

Richard Swedberg,
Berlin, September 2018

Acknowledgements

There would have been no book had there been no contributors. Therefore, we are full of gratitude to David Boje, Barbara
Czarniawska, Kenneth Gergen, Tor Hernes, Geert Hofstede, Edgar
Schein, Andrew Van de Ven and Karl Weick. You all bought into
the book proposal and gave us your time and earnest thoughts on
the topic of theorizing. Also, your encouragement and professional
attitude along the way have been highly inspiring and motivational.
We hope that we do you justice and that you will appreciate the book.

We are also grateful to the late James March and to Mary Jo Hatch
for finding the idea interesting and relevant, and for contributing
with examples of their artistic productions. As such, you illustrate a
shared trait among all contributors – creativity.

A warm appreciation goes to Professor Richard Swedberg who
agreed to write the foreword: a foreword that turned out not only
to present the book but more importantly added ideas alongside
positioning the book in the literature about theorizing.

Two other key players in realizing this book are, of course, our
editors, Francine O'Sullivan and Rachel Downie at Edward Elgar
Publishing. Thanks for being clear in your feedback and for being
positive towards the book proposal and our process.

Thanks to our colleague, Professor Søren Sommer Jagd, for reading
our first manuscript and for valuable feedback in the final spurt.

Finally, we would like to thank Department of Political Science,
Aalborg University and Department of Social Sciences and Business,
Roskilde University, for letting us dive into this book project – which

falls into the category of meta-theoretical reflections and hence was driven by an urge to get wiser while also having fun.

Anne Vorre Hansen and Sabine Madsen
Copenhagen, November 2018

'The Research Ethics' (1974)

The discipline of denial
Is the basis of success

Must I really stop being a man
To be a professor?
Whatinhell is bad
About Whiskey and women?

Research is not for sissies.

Hup.
Hup.
Hup two, three, four.

(Reproduced with the kind permission of James March, 2017)

1. Presentation and premises

I think with them. That, no doubt, is friendship.
(Nicolas Bourriaud, 2002, p. 5)

HOW THE IDEA FOR THE BOOK CAME ABOUT

The idea for this book emerged over the course of a year (or more). Whenever we met for coffee or wine, our talk would – immediately or eventually – come around to work; not just what we were working on, but also *how* we were working. It became clear that we both had an interest in how academic work is carried out in practice and more specifically in the many different work practices and processes that are necessary to accomplish what one wants to realize.

In our experience, many of the practices and processes that constitute academic work are not part of the knowledge that is passed on from seniors to juniors or even talked about in the academic workplace at all. Thus, homemade practices abound; some practices are useful, others less so. Therefore, we had a need for joint reflection on how we work, in order to inspire each other to do things differently and better, or just to feel good about what we were already doing. We believe that other researchers have the same need. The idea for this book is therefore to create a space for the reader to reflect with us and the book's contributors in order to become inspired and feel good about all the ways in which academic work, and more specifically theorizing, can be carried out in practice.

It is easy to explain why we have this common interest in practice. Anne has a background in anthropology and as such she is interested in understanding what people do and how they ascribe meaning to their practice. Sabine has a background in organizational studies and her research centres on understanding how work gets done in organizations, using theory as a tool for uncovering practices that

1

are important for the work, but which may somehow fly under the radar of articulation. Because of our backgrounds and research interests, we see theories as useful analytical lenses and guidelines with which to understand and act in practice. But the main interest in this context is to explore theorizing as a particular type of academic work that involves different work practices and more or less messy processes. But which practices and processes? And more specifically, which practices and processes are *key* to developing interesting and relevant theories that are picked up by the community?

While there are many books and papers that focus on research methods, far fewer resources address theory development as their primary objective. Existing sources typically look at what theory is and what the building blocks of theory ought to be, as well as which steps to take during the theory development process (see, e.g., James Jaccard and Jacob Jacoby, 2009; Richard Swedberg, 2014b; David Whetten, 1989b). And they typically do so by drawing on and synthesizing the author's own experiences as a theorist or editor. In this book we use another approach. Instead of delineating our own experiences and thoughts on how theories are or should be developed, we decided to ask recognized organizational researchers if they were interested in participating in an in-depth interview structured around the following overall question: 'What do you do when you engage in theorizing?' To our great and humble surprise, the contributors to this book replied immediately that they were very interested in talking to us. At this point, the idea took shape and changed from an interesting conversational topic to the more daunting task of writing a book based on the themes and findings that could be gleaned from the interviews.

THE PURPOSE OF THE BOOK: INSPIRATION

Already before we conducted the interviews, the main idea for the book was in place. We wanted to write a book that could inspire the reader to reflect on and develop his or her own practice towards academic theorizing by presenting the breadth and depth of the various both common and different ways of working that recognized organizational researchers use when they engage in thinking processes.

Rather than a normative step-wise approach to what one should do, we had the metaphors of a mirror room and an echo chamber in mind. The metaphors suggest that some practices will stand out and resonate with some readers and not with others – others who will instead see themselves reflected in other ways of working. Thus, the purpose of the book is to provide a foundation from which the reader can pick and choose among the points and practices that are meaningful to them, while discarding the aspects that are not. In that sense, the book prioritizes thematically structured descriptions of actual practice rather than step-wise prescriptions. If the book contains a normative element, it is by making the claim that it is inspiring to deliberately reflect on, discover and actively choose to use a few key practices, among others, that one believes can make a real difference for the way one theorizes.

GETTING READY FOR THEORIZING

When we were conducting the interviews, we realized that the inter-viewees related numerous points, processes and practices that were important for *getting ready for* theorizing, but the actual theorizing remained somewhat elusive, even when we directly prompted them to speak about what they *do* when they theorize. Thus, it seems that the actual doing, or the core of what one does, is very difficult to communicate to others.

Moreover, it seems that theorizing is a much more creative endeavour than systematic, step-by-step approaches are able to elucidate. And because of this, what happens when the researcher theorizes remains somewhat mysterious. However, what is clear is that there are ways of getting in the mood for the creative act of theorizing, making this book about the practices and processes that pave the way for theorizing to happen. Moreover, it is an attempt to shed as much light on the unarticulated aspects of theorizing as possible, through interpretations of the interview data. Hopefully, the book will pro-vide insight into the act of theorizing, that is, into what happens in the space between reaching for a thought and expressing the thought: 'Thinking is pleasurable ... [and] it is the slow, organically growing process of thought involved in writing that lets the ideas emerge in the first place' (Mihaly Csikszentmihalyi, 1991, pp. 126, 131).

THEORY AND THEORIZING

Theory can be seen as the endpoint of theorizing, typically embodied in a text, while theorizing refers to the process that precedes the final text. As Richard Swedberg (2012) states, the two are inherently connected, but currently the emphasis in academia is on the text (and the publication thereof), which in turn means that little is known about the process of theorizing. In this book, we emphasize theorizing rather than theory. We will, of course, mention which theories the interviewees have developed and highlight the several forms that theory, according to the interviewees, can take – from concepts and metaphors to paradigms. However, the purpose is not to present each of the contributors' work, as we primarily are interested in *how* they work. So far, we have used the terms *theory development* and *theorizing* synonymously and we will continue to do so, among other things, for the pragmatic purpose of creating some linguistic variation. However, we favour the term theorizing, because it refers to a process that is happening; in other words, to theory in the making.

THEORIZING AS A LONG-TERM COMMUNAL PROCESS

After we had conducted the interviews, it became clear that the traditional notion of seeing theorizing as a process that culminates with (the publication of) theory as text is somewhat misleading. All the interviewees pointed out, in line with literary theory, that a text only exists if it is read, and, as such, if a theory is relevant for the community and for as long as it is relevant (or when it becomes relevant again), theorizing continues to happen. Thus, this book takes a long-term perspective at theorizing and we highlight that the text is not the endpoint of the theorizing process and that the original author(s) is not the only creator. On the contrary, in order for a theory to be successful, so to speak, it has to be picked up by the community and further developed through communal efforts. Thus, theorizing takes time and people.

THE CHOICE OF INTERVIEWEES

This book is our attempt at theorizing about how organizational researchers develop theory in practice. To help us shed light on that we needed people. We therefore quickly settled on the in-depth individual interview as a suitable method for inquiring into the topic. Thus, as the idea was to interview key thinkers that are well known and widely used by students and researchers in organization studies, we approached a number of people we were fascinated by and who are considered the giants of the field. Most of these replied immediately that they were interested in participating in the project; a few answered that they had retired or no longer gave interviews; and only a few we never heard back from. As such, there is, of course, a selective and pragmatic aspect to the choice of contributors, in the sense that they reflect who we consider key thinkers and those who were interested in participating in the project.

WHAT THE INTERVIEWEES HAVE IN COMMON

The contributors to the book replied that they were interested in participating in an interview because they thought that the book addressed other and novel aspects of theorizing compared to that found in the existing literature on the topic. Their motivation for participating made us realize that even though there is much variety in the contributors' choice of research topics and ways of theorizing – from Kenneth Gergen's focus on generative metaphors to Andrew Van de Ven's emphasis on logical arguments – there are also a number of common denominators.

In general, all contributors have an interest in process. This includes a focus on the processes of the phenomena they are researching, but also, importantly for our purposes, the processes whereby theories are (co-)created. As such, the contributors have in common that they are well versed in the existing literature about theory development and philosophy of science; they are interested in what theory is and what theory can be used for as well as in the process of theorizing; and many of them have contributed journal papers, book chapters, and books on these topics. In addition, the interviewees all refer to curiosity as a personal trait. Many people might describe themselves as curious because it is considered a valuable thing to be. However, curiosity in this case refers to a need for actively seeking out understanding. This means that if there is something the interviewees find interesting, unexpected or novel they turn to the literature and/or go into the field to come to understand. In other words, it is a type of curiosity that leads to explorative action and a search for meaning.

WHO THE INTERVIEWEES ARE

We provide two different types of insight into who the interviewees are, as people and as researchers. In Box 1.1, we present an overview of the eight interviews that were conducted for this book. We describe who we interviewed, how, and what their main research interests are and we provide a quote that captures the essence of each contributor's way of thinking about theorizing. The quotes also serve to highlight some of the themes that are addressed in the book.

In addition to this overview, we present a more personal narrative of each contributor in order to provide insight into the link between the person's background and life story, choice of research topics, and ways of working. The personal narratives can be found in boxes at the end of the chapters, where we present either one or two contributors at a time (see the list of boxes at the beginning of the book to locate the narrative description of each of the contributors).

REFLECTIONS ON GENDER

As mentioned, we have chosen the interviewees based on whom our students, our colleagues, and we are interested in and use in our work. This resulted in more male than female contributors. We found this interesting, because even though we are not gender researchers we are aware of the importance of paying attention to who is talking and who is not; what is being told and what is not; and why this is being told and not something else. In other words, to the classic questions of gender research.

We therefore asked almost all interviewees in a closing remark what it might mean that most of the theories in use in organizational studies

BOX 1.1   OVERVIEW OF THE INTERVIEWEES

Professor David Boje

The interview with David Boje was conducted as a Skype interview from his office at New Mexico State University in Las Cruces, Mexico. David Boje's theorizing focuses on sensemaking, the storytelling organization, and critical inquiry into organizations' use of power. He invented the term 'antenarrative', which refers to a story before it becomes a retrospectively created meaningful whole, that is, before a coherent narrative. 'And you know what, I was teacher of the year for the whole university in my first semester. It was all about the storytelling. This changed the way … I just decided: I am only going to write about storytelling, I am only going to teach storytelling, I am only going to do storytelling.'

Professor Barbara Czarniawska

We conducted the interview with Barbara Czarniawska in person in her office at the University of Gothenburg, Sweden. Barbara Czarniawska's theorizing focuses on processes of organizing, organizational change, fashion and fads in management theories and practice, as well as narratology as a field study technique and analytical lens in organization studies. 'Umberto Eco said many times, metaphors are what we don't know and this is the only thing that is interesting. Facts and names are boring. Metaphors are exactly bisociations, they are putting things together from two different fields. But then, some work and some don't work.'

Professor Kenneth Gergen

The interview with Kenneth Gergen was conducted as a Skype interview from his home in Pennsylvania, United States. Kenneth Gergen's work focuses on social constructionism and the generative aspects of theory and metaphors. He has invented the terms relational being, saturated self and positive ageing, to name a few. 'Once you are a constructionist, you realize that whatever your theory is, your language is going to create that in its terms. It makes the world what it is … You ask a totally different set of questions. You ask "How do I want to create the world and what are the implications of creating it in that way?"'

Professor Tor Hernes

The interview with Tor Hernes was conducted in person in his office at the Copenhagen School of Business, Denmark. Tor Hernes theorizes about organization, time, change and continuity. His work is centred on an event-based understanding of time, inspired by Alfred North Whitehead's philosophy. 'The way I use others [theorists] from outside the organization field, I use them to inspire me, and I sense that I go just to the right depth, so I can say something novel back into my own field, organization studies.'

Professor Emeritus Geert Hofstede

The interview with Geert Hofstede was conducted as a Skype interview from his home in the Netherlands. Geert Hofstede has researched a number of topics, such as how budgets and financial pressures influence people and organizations. However, he is primarily known for his theory about national cultural differences and the dimensions along which the differences can be understood. 'If you ask me what has been the driving force in my work, it was curiosity. It was whenever I came across something that surprised me, to try to find out; how come? ... [and also] in the practical use of my work ... having an impact.'

Professor Emeritus Edgar Schein

The interview with Edgar Schein was conducted as a Skype interview from his home in Palo Alto, United States. Edgar Schein has researched a variety of themes during his career, including indoctrination of prisoners of war, indoctrination in organizations (resulting in the discovery of the concept of career anchors), and organizational culture. Moreover, he has written books about process consultation, humble inquiry, and how to be helpful in practice. '[B]uilding on previous theory is not as important as discovering something that is useful [in practice]. How do we discover something useful? ... the starting point should be experience ... you start with good observations, fieldwork, and interviews, and draw theory out of that.'

Professor Emeritus Andrew Van de Ven

The interview with Andrew Van de Ven was conducted as a Skype interview from his home in Minnesota, United States. Over the course of his academic career, Andrew Van de Ven has worked with group decision-making techniques, organizational assessment methods, organizational change, and innovation processes. Moreover, he has formulated his insights into how to research these themes as a particular research approach labelled 'engaged scholarship'. 'To me to be engaged is not to go alone. Do not do your research, do not do your writing alone, do not do anything alone. Especially when we are addressing problems and questions which are bigger than ourselves.'

Professor Emeritus Karl Weick

The interview with Karl Weick was conducted as a written dialogue. The text is included in this book in full. Karl Weick is one of the founding fathers of the process view in organizational studies, as he early on suggested a shift in perspective from organization to organizing. He is most famous for his writings about sensemaking, which he has studied both with regard to everyday affairs, during disasters and in different types of organizations. 'From the beginning I "played the percentages", figuring that, if I keep writing I can write my way into occasional insights. Long before I heard the phrase, my style was to see what I wrote in order to learn what I thought.'

have been developed by men. In response to this question, Barbara Czarniawska read the following text from one of her book chapters aloud for us:

> In his book *On the Shoulders of Giants*, Robert Merton (1965/1985), declared that ... in historical reality it is the appointed giants who stand on a pyramid of midgets. But it is a demand of the narrative convention that big discoveries must be made by big heroes; a story about ant-like workers would be dull ... I would like to suggest yet another possibility: that of a midget, like myself, who ... suddenly discovers that she was, in fact, all the time standing on somebody's shoulders. Was the reason for invisibility that the shoulders belonged to a female person? (Barbara Czarniawska, 2011, p. 217)

The last line is especially striking as it suggests that female thinkers might play a larger role than we realize, due to taken-for-granted notions that academic heroes are men or simply because their influence goes unacknowledged by both men and women. The other interviewees made similar remarks. Moreover, the shared under-standing was that there are a lot more women in academia now, but it takes a long time before a theory starts to have a widespread impact and therefore it might still be a few years before their theories become well known and widely used.

If gender plays as large a role as gender theory and research suggests, it might be relevant to point out that we are female thinkers and that the insights presented in this book have been created in response to the questions we have asked and based on our interpretations of the provided answers. For this reason, we also believe that it is important that we present our personal narratives in order for the reader to understand our background and how it influences our way of think-ing (see Box 1.2).

BOX 1.2   OUR PERSONAL NARRATIVES

Anne Vorre Hansen

Anne has always had a double side to her: an extrovert and social side and a very quiet introvert one lived out in 'literature escapism'. Since her early childhood she has been reading everything from comic albums/strips such as Yoko Tsuno, Prince Valiant and Tintin to philosophy, crime novels and fiction. The two sides are bridged by a profound curiosity towards stories, be they in literature or in dialogue – based on an urge to explore how stories shape experiences, understandings and future actions. The double-sidedness is also mirrored in Anne's work life, as both a consultant and a researcher with an explicit focus on merging the perceptions of users/citizens/customers with the logic of organizations in innovation processes. The word that best captures her approach and motivation is to 'understand', and especially to understand something better. To Anne this book is therefore motivated by a wish to broaden her horizon and grasp thinking processes more profoundly.

Sabine Madsen

Sabine grew up in a town in Jutland, Denmark, which happened to have a beautiful and well-stocked library. There she discovered the pleasure of being surrounded by words, stories and ideas at an early age, and later the choice of an academic career was not difficult as it allows for the continual recreation of this childhood experience of immersion in words. As a person, Sabine is interested in the many forms in which words can be used to express thought, such as poetry, fiction, non-fiction as well as in literary theory. As a researcher, this translates into an interest in being a part of – and the understanding and creation of – the flow of ideas in circulation in practice, and more specifically in organizations and organizational studies. The word that best captures both her personal and research interest is 'emergence' – the process whereby things such as work practices, theories, works of art and so on come to take the form they do. Thus, writing this book falls directly into the category of a passion project.

REFERENCING PEOPLE

In this book we draw extensively on the interview statements made by the contributors as well as on other authors and theorists, both from the field of organizational studies and beyond. In all cases, we refer to them as people, that is, with their full name. In line with the above-mentioned considerations, we have chosen this referencing style to make the gender of the contributors and authors explicit. Moreover, we do it to remind others and ourselves that it is real people – with real desks, computers, coffee cups, assumptions, interests, likes and dislikes – who develop theories. Thus, before someone is a *giant*, invested with collective meaning and legitimacy that makes him or her larger than human, or a *midget*, an ant-like worker on the academic treadmill, they are first and foremost a person. To read their theory (or their interview statements) is therefore to get a glimpse into that particular person's thinking. Or, as Siri Hustvedt (2016) would say: 'to read is to engage with a trace of someone else's consciousness through a text, which is impregnated with the author's being'.

READING STYLES AND STRATEGIES

This book can be read in different ways and for different inspirational purposes. First of all, it can, of course, be read chronologically from one end to the other. We think of this as a reading strategy that can be coined *the long gaze*. With this strategy, reading takes place over time to grasp the line of thought that is presented in the book as a whole. The term 'the long gaze' also refers to one of the main points of this book, namely that theorizing is more like a marathon than a sprint.

Second, the book can be read one chapter at a time, when the need for inspiration, in general or on a particular topic, arises. We think of this as *the short gaze*, where reading takes place in one sitting – for example, during a commute, to warm up for the day's work, to pass the time in a hopefully pleasant way, and so on. To cater to this type of reading strategy, each chapter addresses one overall theme and has an intro-duction, a middle and an end to ensure a complete reading experience.

Third, the book can be read one text chunk or quote at a time. We think of this as *sampling for sound bites*. With this strategy, reading takes place to become inspired here and now – for example, by opening the book at a random page when in need of fast food for thought, a variation or new tone to one's own writing, or simply a quick distraction. As Kenneth Gergen states: 'I can also get inspired by just reading something. It does not take very much. It depends on the text, but sometimes you can find something pretty quick.' To cater to this type of reading, the content and layout of the book has been designed with many quotes, boxes, informative headlines, as well as with a reader-friendly type and spacing. This might sound trivial but we believe that far more people read books using the sampling strategy than we might normally assume. Yet, most books, and particularly academic books, do not take this into account because content is prioritized over presentation. In this book, we have striven to give equal prioritization to content and layout to support different reading styles, which in turn allows the reader to take away different types of inspiration.

STRUCTURE AND CONTENT OF THE BOOK

The book consists of seven chapters: this introductory chapter, a summary chapter, four content chapters and a 'behind the scenes' chapter, which presents the full interview with Karl Weick. All content chapters follow the same structure. We start each content chapter by introducing the chapter's overall theme and by linking the theme to theoretical concepts of relevance for the subsequent presentation of the empirical findings. The theoretical concepts that set the scene in each chapter have been chosen because they are meaningful to us and because they proved to be useful interpretive devices during our analysis and shared discussions of the interview findings. Thus, we do not provide a comprehensive review of the existing literature or of all the concepts that could be relevant for theorizing in general and for the presented empirical findings. Instead, we use theoretical concepts and references to give the reader a scaffold for understanding the interview findings and to highlight differences and similarities between existing knowledge and our findings.

In addition to theoretical concepts, we use boxes of text as a structural device that allows us to both emphasize key findings from the interviews and challenge established academic notions and expectations, thereby adding extra meaning to the text. Thus, we use boxes in (at least) four different ways:

- to present the personal narratives of the contributors;
- to provide more detail on some of the theoretical concepts and work practices that the contributors point out as particularly important for theorizing;

- to present longer quotes from the interview material, where the contributors tell a story, give examples of how they work or delineate their line of reasoning;
- to describe anecdotes from the interview situations and from our own experiences as researchers, teachers and supervisors.

After mentioning these structural aspects, we now provide an overview description of the content of the remainder of the book. The logic of the chapters' sequence is that we start in Chapter 2 by exploring how the contributors engage in theorizing and how the groundwork for thinking is conditioned by personal inspiration and practices. Subsequently, in Chapter 3, we dig further into the unit of analysis, trying to expose what it means to look at something and what this looking is motivated by. Then, in the 'intermezzo' chapter 'Behind the Scenes – Interviewing Karl Weick', we explore one of the particularly salient theorizing practices, namely writing. To this end, we present the written interview with Karl Weick in full. This chapter will be the foundation for Chapter 4, where we turn towards the literature base and academic antecedents, recognizing that knowledge production is deeply anchored in history and social processes. In Chapter 5, we zoom out and focus on perceptions of what it means to make a theoretical contribution. Last, in the final chapter, Chapter 6, we sum up key points and practices across interviews and chapter discussions – before leaving the reader to do his or her own thinking and theorizing.

WHAT THE BOOK HAS TO OFFER

With this book we have written the book we wanted to read, but also the book that we wanted to write. Thus, the book provides:

- insights from interviews with key thinkers in the field of organization studies (what they *are* doing and what works for them, rather than what one *should* be doing);
- a focus on aspects that make theorizing a much more personal and meaningful endeavour than just getting published;
- descriptions of different types of work practices and understandings of what the work entails, from Karl Weick's very concrete everyday descriptions of how he starts his writing day

to Kenneth Gergen's outline of how his academic goals and approaches to theorizing have changed over the course of his career.

We hope that the book can inspire the reader to engage in theorizing, not only as an instrumental work task but also as an existential urge to understand and create new meaning, especially since all contributors have been able to balance between being a human and a professor, as explicated in the poem by James March at the beginning of this book. It might be that 'research is not for sissies', but it certainly seems to be for creative collaborative people with a well-developed sense of humour.

Box 1.3 presents the research approach that we have used to collect and analyse the empirical interview data, which constitutes the foundation for this book.

BOX 1.3   THE RESEARCH APPROACH

This book is primarily based on data from eight in-depth interviews. The interviews were structured around an interview question guide (see the Appendix to this book) that we sent to the interviewees beforehand. This was done for two reasons. First, it would allow the interviewees to prepare for the interview if they wished to. All interviewees did. Second, it would help with potential language barriers during the interview as they also had the questions in writing.

The interviews were conducted in person, via Skype, or as written dialogue. The oral interviews lasted approximately an hour and a half. They were sound-recorded and subsequently transcribed verbatim. All interviews were conducted in the period from mid-August 2017 to mid-September 2017.

After the interviews had been transcribed verbatim, we made what we would refer to as 'analytical transcripts'. The aim was to make the interviews as reader friendly as possible, by presenting the text according to the themes that the interviewee talked about, deleting repetitions that did not add to the meaning, making conjunctions in places to ensure more fully formed sentences, and by presenting the text in a readable, clear font. Making the analytical transcripts was therefore a first very preliminary round of analysis. Moreover, it was meant as a gift to the interviewees, providing them with a reader-friendly text that presented the meaning they created during the interview.

The analytical transcripts were sent to the interviewees for approval. All interviewees took time to go through the transcripts, fix mistakes we had made, and to polish the text to convey the meaning of their thinking better. This meant that the transcripts lost some of their spoken quality, and instead became very well-written accounts of the interviewees' thinking about theorizing. This book is based on these corrected and approved transcripts that have been generated through several phases of dialogue, listening, analysis, writing and rewriting. We considered this process important in order to create and collate data for the book as well as possible.

After the data had been created we read through the interview transcripts, identified the main themes, and outlined the structure of the book based on these themes. This can be considered a compositional analysis. Next, we carried out a more detailed analysis of what the content of each chapter should be and this was written down as themes and keywords that captured what we wanted to cover in the particular chapter. After this, another round of analysis was conducted during the writing process. When we started writing one of the content chapters we began with reading the transcripts from the perspective of the overall theme and theoretical concepts of the chapter. Based on this, key findings and selected quotes were included in the already existing detailed outline of the chapter structure – in some cases, resulting in a reworking of the initially delineated chapter themes and sub-themes. Last, the actual writing took place, with one of us as the main author of the first draft. The draft was then revised by both of us until we were satisfied that we had managed to express what we wanted to.

BOX A   BARBARA CZARNIAWSKA – THE PERSONAL NARRATIVE

Barbara was born in 1948 in Poland into a family of graphomaniacs; her three brothers and herself have all published books. The need to write is also reflected in Barbara's early desire to become a journalist.

In Poland, at the time of Barbara's adolescence, it seemed obvious to get a university education, and also it was imperative to have a master's degree to study journalism. Barbara chose to study psychology, but before she graduated she realized that being a journalist in a communist country was a bit more complicated than expected. Therefore, when she got a PhD offer from two professors after her master's, she accepted. Since there were many candidates in social psychology, the professors decided on her behalf that she would become a doctoral student in industrial psychology. Barbara defended her dissertation in economics and psychology in 1976 at the Warsaw School of Economics and subsequently she worked at the Faculty of Psychology.

In 1981, Barbara got a Fellowship from American Council of Learned Societies (ACLS) at MIT Sloan School of Management. Shortly afterwards, however, martial law was imposed in Poland, which meant that she was not allowed to stay in the States. Barbara wanted to do field studies and she therefore went to Berlin, which two years after became a platform for moving to Stockholm's School of Economics as a visiting scholar, where she stayed until 1990. Then, after five years in Lund, she came to Gothenburg, which is now the place where she has lived and worked for the longest period in her life. The history of moving and the focus on field studies seem to be a red thread in Barbara's life, and hence her research. She has physically been moving from one place to another, and, theoretically, she has been jumping back and forth from one discipline to another, namely psychology, economics, management and literature. This multi-movement also relates to her approach to the field – for example, Barbara has both focused on doing field studies but also on how to do field studies, approaching field study methodology as a field in itself.

Barbara's dynamic attitude is reflected in her perception of her academic work life. She stresses that she has experienced the necessary conditions to pursue the things she found interesting and that she is good at. Summing up, the most thrilling thing about being in academia is, in her opinion: irregularities.

2. Engaging in theorizing

> It is by no means obvious where the ontological boundary between
> theoretical and atheoretical lies!
> (Martin Heidegger, 1927 [2010], p. 341)

In this chapter, we explore the grey zone between the concept of theorizing and the act of theorizing. We present the contributors' reflections on what theory is, what it means (to them as individuals) to theorize, and how they support thinking processes via personal practices and inspiration. Thus, the chapter provides insight into the subjective and social aspects of theorizing, with the aim of outlining a process-oriented and engaging approach.

SETTING THE SCENE

We start out in ancient Greek philosophy, which still provides some of the cornerstones for how we currently view knowledge production, especially with regard to what constitutes valid knowledge. To exemplify, the modern understanding of theory and theorizing is based on concepts such as *science* and *reason* (Patrick Jackson, 2010), which are highly inspired by the metaphysics of Aristotle. This implies the precedence of theoretical thinking over practical knowledge, which in turn means that the subject becomes an observer and the world the object to be studied. The relation between object and subject, between body and mind, has been central in the continuous philosophical debate since René Descartes – a debate that is still the foundation for different approaches to knowledge production today (ibid.).

In general, there are two different approaches to knowledge production: the dualist and the monist. The dualist position accepts the division between the subject and the world, stressing that the only thing we as humans can know for certain is our own existence based on our thinking (Justus Hartnack and Johannes Sløk, 1996, p. 141).

From this perspective, the epistemological stance relates to how this 'knowing' subject obtains reliable knowledge about the world, which exists outside the subject and which therefore is mind-independent. In contrast to this, the monist position rejects the division between the subject and the world. Following this, the view on epistemology is that what needs to be explicated is how knowledge production is constitutive for the world itself, leaving the researcher inherently part of the object under study. In this book, we look at theorizing from a monist perspective. With our feet firmly rooted in this perspective, we see the researcher as someone who is actively *engaged* – through his or her attention, efforts, passions and personality – in theorizing about the world.

With regard to how knowledge is produced, there are also two different approaches: the nomothetic/positivist and the ideographic/ interpretive approach. Theorizing from a positivist view seeks to uncover universal causalities and correlations based on empirical observations. This is founded on a *natural science* tradition, and hence a nomothetic science ideal, where the truth about phenomena is out there in the world to be explored and revealed (Egon Guba and Yvonna Lincoln, 1982). In contrast, the ideographic ideal focuses on ideas and on understanding *human reality*, which are not observable as such since they are based on abstractions and unfolded inter-subjectively and therefore always subject to interpretation. In this chapter, we use the distinction between nomothetic and ideographic research to shed light on the contributors' different ways of thinking about theory. Moreover, both authors and the contributors have a primarily ideographic approach to knowledge production, with a knowledge interest that centres on understanding a particular part of the world, namely the slice of human reality that we call organizations and organization studies.

Jeffrey Edwards and John Berry (2010) state that the nomothetic/ positivist perception of theorizing, and therefore the quest to discover causalities and correlations, prevails. Through a review (ibid.) they show that, for example, the *Academy of Management Journal* requires authors to make theoretical contributions to each submission, which leads to a discipline that primarily develops theories based on directional statements (ibid.). Jeffrey Edwards and John Berry argue that this is based on the assumption that theory is an end in itself.

In contrast to this view, we in this book all share the understanding that Karl Weick presented in his paper from 1995 – that focusing on the process of theorizing is as important as focusing on theory as outcome, leading to the claim that theory might be the process rather than the product (Karl Weick, 1995a, p. 385). One way to interpret Karl Weick's statement is to see the strength of a theory as its 'intellectually utility' more than its descriptive accuracy or normative evaluation towards what is being studied (Patrick Jackson, 2010). This view is supported by Henry Mintzberg (2005, p. 3), who writes:

> So we need all kinds of theories – the more, the better. As researchers, scholars and teachers, our obligation is to stimulate thinking … Our students and readers should leave our classrooms and publications pondering, wondering, thinking – not knowing.

From this perspective, theory is not an outcome in itself, nor a truth about objects that can be found 'out there' in reality. Instead, theory is an analytical construct that is created by the writer to stimulate the reader's thinking and to invite the reader to participate in theorizing. And as all writers are also readers, it seems promising to view theory as an ongoing process of collaborative theorizing, with no fixed starting or endpoint.

WHAT IS THEORY?

Despite differences in scope and weighting, all contributors apply a process perspective to the notion of theory. They are all concerned with the issue of what a theory is and what a theory does, but their main interest lies in the process of thinking, and in thinking further, rather than advocating for a specific theory or for their own analytical concepts as fixed ideas. This openness towards ideas and terms is mirrored in their understanding, or definition, of theory. The interviews reveal a variety of definitions, making it interesting to explore these different perceptions, or discursive constructions, of what theory is.

For Andrew Van de Ven, theory plays an important role in organizational studies. He refers to a theory as a logical claim, a proposition based on the process of theorizing – making theory the substance and theorizing the process of getting there. In that sense he is close to the dictionary (*Merriam-Webster*) definition of theory as principles, by accepting that there is an outcome of the process of theorizing. Yet, as he advocates and has conducted longitudinal research he is as interested in the process as in the outcome.

On the opposite end of the continuum, Edgar Schein resists the notion of theory, arguing that we are still in a pre-theory stage since we as researchers in social sciences apply rather fuzzy (but fortunately important) concepts, mental models and assumptions. Similarly, Tor Hernes states that 'we do not really work with theories' in the same way or for the same purpose as the more compartmentalized natural sciences. Instead, he finds it more accurate to say that organizational researchers use analytical concepts that might be drawn from different disciplines to understand organizations and the field of organization studies better.

Barbara Czarniawska agrees with both Edgar Schein and Tor Hernes, but she is more concerned with metaphors. She likes the metaphor of theory as a plot and she sees herself as a detective when engaging in theorizing. Her view is that theory is a pattern that emerges from the structuring of associations and bisociations. As such, theory materializes due to mental structuring processes that you can only to some extent condition: 'You have to pack in things in your mind, but then to let them be.' Karl Weick also sees theory as a pattern that emerges particularly through writing, and when the pattern seems to exist it can be called a name. It is due to the use of *new* names, metaphors and concepts that new understandings can develop – and it is these new understandings of the phenomenon under study that are interesting, not the theory in itself.

Kenneth Gergen, in a social constructivist manner, leaves the mental processes behind, and focuses more on the room for dialogue in which assumptions and new ways of understanding can be socially constructed. This leads to the understanding of theory as an open space to be interactively explored. To some extent, theory as an open space resonates with David Boje's approach to theory. He rejects the idea of a fixed theory and puts in its place what he refers to as ontological alternatives. The main point is to go back to philosophical basics and to be existentially concerned with *being*, that is, with how we as humans are in the world.

In summary, each of the contributors has their own definition of theory, which in turn leads them to favour a particular form in which to express their thinking – ranging from logical claims, analytical concepts, metaphors, and to the exposure of assumptions about the research topic and the human condition in general. The personal and/or professional reasons for these varied manifestations invite reflections on one's own approach to theory and understanding of what theory is, does, and stimulates.

WHAT THEORY AIMS AT

Despite the mentioned differences in the approach to the concept of theory, the contributors agree that one of the main functions of theory is to *reduce complexity*. However, a key issue is that reducing complexity is not the same as a theory being true. Since most contributors are deeply anchored in ideographic science perceptions and abductive practices, they are not concerned with being right or wrong. Instead, they are concerned with creating a foundation for thinking and with looking for connections that are meaningful. As Geert Hofstede states:

> Be careful with dimensions! Dimensions do not exist. Dimensions are only there in your mind. Dimensions are a way in which you – in a complex world which is simply too complex to find your way – you divide, you find directions in that. But it does not mean that it is the only way that you can divide this complex world.

In the same vein, Barbara Czarniawska comments that the desire to make theory in bullets points, or to find what she refers to as algorithms for organizational processes, does nothing more than act as a tranquillizer to reduce anxiety. In that sense they serve a legitimate purpose, but they are not theory in the sense of supporting or triggering thinking processes. Nor do they encourage the act of actually thinking further and beyond what is already there, which is what the contributors aim at.

In Box 2.1 Tor Hernes describes how he conceives of theory and why he thinks it is important to distinguish between meaningful connections and causality.

BOX 2.1   MEANINGFUL CONNECTIONS VERSUS
           CAUSALITIES

Tor Hernes states: 'We don't really work with theories ... A theory, I think,
shows causalities ... but I don't really believe much in causalities ... What we
do is search for meaningful connections. This is my job as a teacher – I teach
philosophy of science here. Students come to the first semester from their
bachelor's degree, and they tend to have this causality view: if I do this as
a manager, then that will happen. It is my job to tell them that it is not going
to happen. We don't know, and even those who pretend to know, really don't
know. But it takes a semester at least to get them accustomed to that idea
that you have to do your own interpretation. That is where the theoretical
frameworks come in.'

THINKING FURTHER

To think further is a core concept when it comes to understanding
what the organizational researcher does when engaged in theorizing.
With this concept the understanding of theorizing shifts from seeing
the use of existing theories, collection of empirical data and so on
as the main activities to seeing them as ingredients (albeit important
ones), or as stepping stones to think with – and importantly beyond.
Thus, it is when the researcher uses what already exists as tools
to clarify and express his or her thinking using names, concepts,
metaphors and so on that are personally meaningful and new to the
particular research field that theorizing takes place.

However, to put yourself and your thinking out there in this way is
not without risk. Thus, an aspect of thinking beyond existing theories, concepts and frameworks seems to be tension, contradiction
and criticism. This emphasizes that research and therefore theorizing
is not happening in the abstract, but is part of a social field. This can
both be seen as being engaged with others or enacted as a game of
contestation.

Andrew Van de Ven stresses that it is imperative 'not to go alone'.
The claim is based on the understanding that if you want to research
big and important topics, you need to collaborate with others and

that it is in the interplay between different and contradictory viewpoints and arguments that new realizations emerge. Another way of going further is illustrated by Kenneth Gergen's story of how early in his career he challenged the field: 'It was partly a game of chess, but it was challenging the field saying, "Hey, I can play this piece, what can you do about that?"' Even though he meant to challenge existing assumptions, he was surprised by the immense criticism he was met with – which was nevertheless important, because it challenged his thinking and made him refine his arguments. Thus, despite the criticism, he continued his research but later on in his career he become more focused on using unexamined assumptions as a point of departure for proposing positive alternatives. Kenneth Gergen stresses that he experienced this shift in focus from being a challenger to also coming up with genuine alternatives as a far more constructive approach.

As you can tell from our interview question guide in the Appendix to this book, we asked the interviewees if students are 'allowed' to challenge theory. We have been quite puzzled ourselves with the reluctance among students to engage in a theoretical dialogue with the theories they apply – both in working with our own students and in our jobs as external examiners. Since critical reflections, at least in the case of Denmark, are prevalent in learning objectives across educational institutions, we are a bit bothered about students mainly doing more or less explicit hypothesis testing. Thus, we are quite delighted that we prospectively, now standing on the shoulders of giants (!), are able to say to students and young researchers that they are not only allowed to, in fact they are encouraged to, continuously contest and negotiate theory – not for the sake of criticism but for the sake of clarifying their own thinking and creating new ideas and understandings.

Box 2.2 presents our anecdotal reflection on the interview situations, where it was very apparent to us that the contributors had spent their lives sharpening their ability to think and to explain their thinking.

BOX 2.2 THINKING FASTER

A mutual friend of ours once said that she, after her PhD, could feel how her analytical skills were sharpened and that she was able to think faster than before. Her statement came back to us during the interviews. It was extremely apparent in the interview situation that the contributors are thinkers and that they have been using their brains professionally for many years. We have both conducted many interviews in our work life, but we have never experienced that the interviewee had the themes of the interview in mind to the same degree as us. Also, it was clear that the interviewees had been reflecting on the questions beforehand and that they managed to keep a structure in their head alongside juggling with many different themes at a time – never losing track of the themes they introduced themselves. More than once we were stunned by the ability of the interviewees to take a long detour just to come back to the main point minutes later. To become sharp and fast thinkers like the contributors is motivational to us in itself.

THE BEAUTY OF THEORY

For a theory to live, an audience is needed. The contributors therefore state that theory needs to be appealing – an aspect that became a recurring theme throughout the interviews. Analysing the interviews, it seems that a theory is appealing when it says something profound and when it is perceived as complete.

Thus, some of the contributors stress the beauty of a well-considered framework. They put weight on the aesthetic aspect of appealing theories, underscoring how creative thinking is linked to the ability to express yourself in a profound and poetic manner. This has also been a concern of the late James March, who embraces beauty as a human aspiration, emphasizing a sort of double move – that being aesthetically ambitious sets the ground for beautiful ideas to emerge. He states:

> Scholarship celebrates ideas, and in that celebration it honors beauty not only as an instrument of utility but also as a fundamental human aspiration. The scholar who seeks beauty in ideas, despite the unbearable lightness of the search – or perhaps because of it – affirms an essential element of humanity. (James March, 2013, p. 9)

At least in our experience, the notion of beauty is seldom made explicit when talking about theorizing, but we both immediately understood what the thinkers referred to. This might have to do with the condition that we all know what beauty is when we see it but also that beauty is subjectively determined. This is where resonance enters the scene. Thus, all contributors describe how they have met or stumbled upon an idea, a metaphor or a thought that they simply *liked* or that seemed to mirror their own thoughts – as when Kenneth Gergen discovered Ludwig Wittgenstein:

> Finding Wittgenstein was not like, wow this is so well written. It is not. It is strangely written, but it was what I was already kind of thinking and Wittgenstein said it, and extended it in ways and really took it far. It was finding the voice that was already there. Now I am partly making up that voice too.

Tor Hernes also recalls the feeling when he began reading Bruno Latour: 'It is very seductive. It rings a bell, it just sounds true in a sense!' This is backed up by Barbara Czarniawska, who recounts how she wrote and thanked a theorist because of his 'beautiful piece against narrativity', due to the feeling of being mirrored. She adds an account of how she tested one of her own expressions, 'ergonography', with a colleague who thought the term would never catch on with an audience because he perceived it to be too ugly. She dryly remarks: 'He was right.'

Where Kenneth Gergen, Tor Hernes and Barbara Czarniawska explicitly emphasize beauty and attraction as both something to be drawn towards and something to strive for, others are inspired by the lingo of the academic field they are schooled or working within. To exemplify, we asked Edgar Schein how the focus on cultural layers came about, and the prompt answer was: 'I get it straight out of anthropology. I am using the anthropological model of culture.' Asking Geert Hofstede the same question, but on dimensions, he just as quickly replied: 'Well, the reason I called them dimensions is that I was trained as an engineer. Obviously, an engineer sees things three-dimensionally.' In this manner, the interviewees stress that in developing analytical concepts and theoretical frameworks they draw on the work of others as well as the terminologies of their field(s). An aspect that underscores that knowledge production, and therefore theorizing, is not a process detached from the context in which it takes place.

ENGAGING IN DIALOGUE WITH YOURSELF AND OTHERS

During the interviews it struck us how much theorizing is about being at play as a person. This is one of the reasons that, besides the point that the contributors have some interesting life stories to tell, we integrated personal narratives in this book. When we as audience read theory, we seldom take into account that it is built upon underlying assumptions of the theorists – and that they not only bring theoretical reflections and syntheses to the table, but also personal viewpoints and perceptions. In that manner, the basis of the theoretical contribution is to be found in the interplay between the way you are as a person in the world and the subject of the research. Or, returning to the philosophical introduction to the chapter, the personal ontological and existential stands frame the knowledge produced. An interesting note here is that the abductive approach of the contributors is not only applied as a research method but also as an existential epistemological approach. As such, thinking processes are perceived iteratively in the sense that you engage in dialogue with your own ideas and preconceptions as well as with those of others; not to prove yourself right, but to have new thoughts and expand your horizon. As such, theorizing might be seen as a process continuously merging intra-subjective and inter-subjective dialogues. Or as Edgar Schein states: 'There is no such thing as pure individuality. It is always in relation to something else. So, when we talk about "the personality" we have to specify in relation to what.' Thus, there might be a substantial relation between theory/theorizing and the personal approach – among other things due to different pre-understandings, different research goals and different ways of engaging in theorizing.

DIFFERENT WAYS OF ENGAGING IN THEORIZING

We have identified the following ways of theorizing, which are, of course, highly intertwined:

- *Talking.* Kenneth Gergen underlines that thinking and theorizing are dialogical in nature, implying that interaction with an audience, be that inside or outside academia, influences both the existing thoughts and the thoughts to come: 'When you are asked a question by various audiences and when you hear yourself respond to those questions you realize: wow, that is a whole new thing, there are several things that I have not thought about.' This aspect of dialogue is reflected in most interviews.
- *Listening.* As Andrew Van de Ven reflects: 'Maybe the most important for scholars is to listen, but we do not listen very well. We tend to talk.' The point of Andrew Van de Ven's statement is dualistic. First, listening is perceived to be the foundation for creativity to emerge, and second, listening is understood as a personal trait of being open towards what the phenomenon under study 'says' something about.
- *Reading.* Another integrated aspect of theorizing is reading, and thinking with literature. Tor Hernes in a very illustrative manner took an old book down from the shelves and let us smell it while he was explaining why he entered academia and still loves to be here. Barbara Czarniawska also stressed that 'literature is the true love of my life', and despite this being related to fiction she emphasizes how academia has been a platform for sneaking her passion for literature into her own writing.
- *Writing.* In a sense, the process of writing is where thoughts and realizations most concretely manifest themselves. However, as Karl Weick stresses, the process of writing is entangled with the process of realization. In other words, theorizing takes place as the full argument unfolds during the process of (re) writing and revising.

The above list identifies how personal characteristics, such as being a conversationalist, a (good) listener, a literature addict, a writer and/or a thinker, shape the engagement in theorizing. Based on these more overall reflections and approaches to theory and theorizing we will now zoom in on practices that condition the thinking itself.

CREATING CONDITIONS FOR THINKING

All contributors perceive thinking and theorizing as highly creative processes and they see themselves as creative people. In our experience, this sort of artistic approach, and trait, does not seem to be specifically articulated when junior researchers are urged to develop theory. But, as a natural consequence of being and feeling creative, almost all theorists have an artistic side to them – Geert Hofstede used to play the guitar, David Boje and Edgar Schein draw and sketch, Kenneth Gergen (especially in his early days) wrote poems, whereas others simply refer to great thinkers as doing art. And as the poem by James March and the cover illustration for this book by Mary Jo Hatch reveal, they too are artists. Without indulging in over-analysing, it might be fair to state that to get inspiration from various sources and to play in domains other than academia enhances the ability to cross-pollinate thoughts and ideas.

Like most contributors, Andrew Van de Ven underlines that you need a catalyst for creativity to happen. For example, he has a practice of attending classes outside his own research domain and he also stresses the practice of reading broadly as a foundation for thinking further: 'Broadminded, broadly-read people are more likely to be creative than are narrowly-read people.' Also, Barbara Czarniawska suggests that you need to have enough books in your mental library to actually be able to associate with something – but still finding the balance so you do not have so many that you end up associating with everything! In Edgar Schein's terms, this sort of influence is referred to as serendipity since it is not necessarily based on concrete choices or actions, but is rather fluent and emerging based on your personal knowledge base.

A focus on literature as a foundation for thinking and hence for writing is evident in all interviews, and especially the urge to go back in history seems to prevail. For some it is getting inspired by the approach of the founding fathers of the research field – as Tor Hernes stresses: 'Being an academic to me is working incessantly to try and write something that is simple and profound. That is what Jim March does. Jim is a master of it, he is a poet in our field.' Likewise, Karl Weick and Andrew Van de Ven mention James March and Herbert Simon, and David Boje, Tor Hernes and Barbara Czarniawska refer to Karl Weick as both an inspiration and a sparring partner in their early careers. Most contributors also read and get inspiration from classic philosophy – from Plato and Aristotle to Martin Heidegger, Ludwig Wittgenstein and Mikhail Bakhtin. Hence, there seems to be a shared experience of going back and realizing that everything is already there to be drawn upon. David Boje states: 'I got this strong notion that these philosophers [e.g., Plato] actually had a better understanding of the world than any current issue of any academy journal.' Finally, the personal history of thinking, manifested in one's own publications, or in life-long reading of poetry, fiction and novels, can serve as an inspirational trigger.

These different notes on history highlight what in a broad sense inspires the thinkers. The next step is to look into concrete actions when engaging in theorizing, that is, the process of writing down your thoughts, or in Kenneth Gergen's words: 'There you play around like you would if you were writing a poem: "that does not go well, or that does not feel right, or that is not aesthetic, or that does not clang".'

The contributors account for different practices that support their thinking processes. The practices might be both deliberate actions taken based on personal experience or merely articulated as an afterthought based on the interview question. In that manner, the platform for thinking consists of both conditional practices such as routines and of the more fluid notion of being in a specific state of mind. In particular, getting in the right mood reveals some interest- ing and inspirational practices. As mentioned, to some it is to read broadly, whereas moving or doing things other than focusing on thinking works for others: 'I think best when I move in different con- texts. I can be sitting down, I can be running, I can be hiking, cycling, lying in my bed, cooking. But it's more the shift between things that I do' (Tor Hernes). And then, going from thinking to writing, most contributors relate how they have figured out what works well for them – which can be to write from the early morning, to schedule writing time and be very strict with it, or to read in the language that you are going to write in. For Barbara Czarniawska, another way of getting in the mood for writing is to read *belles lettres* – small, beautifully written texts focusing on the aesthetic value of the piece more than the content.

In sum, the picture is that reading and writing are intertwined practices that fruitfully add to the creative process of theorizing. Even though no best-practice formula can be revealed, it seems key to find your own practice and actually think of it as such, thereby giving authority to and creating a space for your own thinking.

In Box 2.3, Barbara Czarniawska reflects on creativity using the concepts of association and bisociation.

BOX 2.3 THE PUZZLE OF CREATIVITY

Barbara Czarniawska reflects: 'Again, thanks to my psychology studies I believe that the answers to the puzzle of creativity are two. One is association and the other is bisociation, as Koestler called it. Bisociation associates elements from completely different fields, and that is usually how invention starts. You cannot programme it, though many try to. Hans Selye, the guy who invented the term stress, said that he usually read serious stuff before going to sleep and in the morning very often he had the answers. And it happens to me quite often too. What is worse, sometimes the whole night is too long. Sometimes I have to write it out in the middle of the night, so I don't continue to do editing in my head.'

BARRIERS TO THINKING

Now that we have looked at inspiration and how the contributors create conditions for thinking, let us move on to barriers to thinking. The contributors were all very honest in this regard and disclose how barriers to thinking can both be related to concrete aspects such as lack of time, getting distracted or simply being uninspired, whereas a more profound barrier is related to the fear of not 'getting there'. The term anxiety, or 'angst', emerged in most interviews. There is the existential anxiety of making the wrong decisions or to doubt yourself and your abilities. This can be related to the influential decisions concerning your work life, which Edgar Schein referred to as inspired choices – for example, to do a PhD or not – or as a more profound fear with no direct object. Additionally, there is a more external anxiety concerning feedback, reviews, and the reception of your work. This anxiety occurs when you let these concerns about external evaluation influence your thinking process.

But as much as anxiety is perceived to be a barrier, some also consider it a trigger. David Boje tells a very honest story about how he as a junior researcher was told that he was the worst teacher and the worst writer the faculty had ever seen: 'It shattered my self-esteem. And it was not good to begin with. But the thing it did do was it freaked me out in an important way. I just started doing my own thing, instead of trying to do everybody else's thing', and eventually the teaching scores rose and the writing improved. To address these different sorts of anxiety, Tor Hernes and Barbara Czarniawska provide some fruitful observations on knowing and trusting yourself. Barbara Czarniawska stresses that you need to diagnose yourself so you know both what you are good at and what you are not good at. And then her recommendation is to go with what you are good at and collaborate with others with a different profile from yourself to complement your competences. Somewhat similarly, Tor Hernes emphasizes the need to have a strong 'habitus', which he refers to as the ability to shut things out so they do not distract your creative process. The story of David Boje illustrates very well how building up a strong habitus and a high degree of self-awareness can be a driver for doing your 'own' thing. And to all of us who have experienced destructive reviews, or what sometimes simply seems like rude feedback, it is a good reminder that stamina and self-esteem should make you trust your gut feeling and basic ideas.

It might be clear by now that inspiration and the process of theorizing is perceived as a highly subjective matter, which is why all theorists are disinclined to make recommendations. They seem reluctant to offer tips and tricks concerning theorizing, since the main recommendation, when pushed a little by us, is that you must find your own personal way in academia. Nevertheless, we dare pass on the following pieces of advice:

> For the juniors you know, find your own voice. Find your writing style. Find your muse. The thing that is inspiring to you – and just stick to it. (David Boje)

> The problem is to have voice right? If you don't have that, you have the reviewers' voice. If you don't have your own project your voice will be

your supervisor's voice. But when you are out there, after your PhD and if you are lucky to have a postdoc or if you are going to be an assistant professor we are looking for someone with a voice. It can be a weak voice, but a voice nevertheless. (Tor Hernes)

Being a junior faculty, how would you approach the giants? I would say: read carefully and historically. We cannot step into a field saying I know it better. Instead, you have to build on and show why what has been done is right or wrong. Building on the giants is not to agree with them, it is to read them systematically and carefully. (Andrew Van de Ven)

In Box 2.4 we elaborate on the concept of voice as several contributors stress that finding and using your own voice is an important aspect of theorizing.

SUMMARY

This chapter has revealed a variety of understandings of theory and ways of theorizing. A key point is that the contributors all have their personal take on what theory is and that they have found the theorizing practices and writing style that allows them to express their thinking. It seems to be the combination of their choice of research topic inspired by their backgrounds and passions; their way of thinking about this topic, aided by existing theories that resonate with them; and their preferred way of expressing their thinking that gives them a unique voice. Thus, this chapter shows that theorizing that has the potential to resonate with others is deeply personal, because it is the personal take on the research topic that creates new meaning. It is therefore also important to notice that the contributors stress that it takes time and courage to find your own voice and to stick to what you want to do and say – also in the face of criticism. Thus, the summary, based on the contributors' and our reflections, would be to dare to find your own approach to theorizing, and as a very important part thereof – your own voice.

However, theorizing is not only an individual task. It is also a social process where the researcher in dialogue with both humans and literature becomes more knowledgeable on the phenomena that called on him or her to think in the first place. From this perspective,

---

BOX 2.4   THE CONCEPT OF VOICE

As has become clear, several contributors emphasize both the importance of finding your own voice as a theorist and voice as an important criterion for academic recruitment and promotion. However, the concept of voice is ambiguous. Here we look at a number of definitions to inspire the reader to reflect on what voice is and how to find one's own.

One way of defining voice in academia is to focus on the writer's ability to give voice to others. This often refers to qualitative and/or critical research, where the researcher aims to let the viewpoints, experiences and concerns of minority groups (e.g., with regard to class, gender and sexual orientation), certain employee groups or overlooked aspects of leadership (e.g., managerial uncertainty and vulnerability) be heard in academic texts. As such, developing an individual voice can be related to the writer's choice to take a critical stand and to give certain people and their experiences priority.

Another way to define voice is to focus less on what is said and more on how it is said – for example, by looking at how the writer builds an argument, conjoins existing ideas, and uses the academic genre to express his or her own thinking.

Yet another way to understand voice is to differentiate between texts that deliberately try to have no voice and texts that have a unique voice. The first category encompasses writing where 'objectivity' or neutrality is prioritized, thereby hiding the subjective viewpoints and choices of the author. The second category refers to texts that have a unique voice because the words of the text both fit the writer yet also resonate with the reader. According to this definition, a unique voice is a phenomenon that is co-created by the writer and the reader.

These distinctions and definitions regarding the concept of voice can be used for reflecting on and developing one's own voice by: taking a stand, striving to convey the voice of others, focusing on how one writes, and by carefully choosing the words that you feel capture the essence of the topic under study – which may or may not resonate with the reader.

Source: Inspired by Peter Elbow (1998) and Jay Parini (2008).

---

existing theories are invitations to engage in theorizing and theorizing is the act of using what already exists to think further.

Hence, if we think further based on insights from this chapter, we suggest that theorizing can be seen as a continual insistence on creating profound ways of understanding a dynamic world, for the benefit of oneself and others. This implies two things – that theory is always in the making and that researchers are actively and collaboratively engaged in creating this dynamic world through their expressed understandings thereof.

BOX B   TOR HERNES – THE PERSONAL NARRATIVE

Tor was born in 1957 in Norway. Already as a boy he loved writing, inspired by his mother who was a teacher of Norwegian. Tor links his passion for writing, and talking in front of people, to his positive experience of having an academic work life. He entered into academia when he was 38 years old, having created a family and built up a one-man consultancy business before that.

Originally, Tor started out as a civil engineer wanting to build bridges. In his early career, he worked for an engineering company in the UK, which subsequently led to a job for the United Nations where he travelled around Asia and Africa. But he wanted the freedom of being a consultant and hence became freelance. During this period, he was encouraged to do a PhD due to his ability to come up with good ideas. Tor did not have a master's degree, but it turned out that at Lancaster University in the UK it was possible to get enrolled as a master's student and upgrade to a PhD. He commuted to Lancaster and obtained his PhD degree in organization and management in 1995.

Afterwards, Tor became an associate professor at Tromsø University where he worked for four years before going to the Norwegian Business School in Oslo in 1999. In addition to giving lectures on his work at universities around Europe and the States, Tor is now both a professor in organization and management at the Norwegian School of Management, Oslo and professor of organization theory at Copenhagen Business School in Denmark.

What got Tor hooked on the academic life was his love for literature, an inclination for searching and the thrill of discovering. This is deeply intertwined with an urge to avoid dualisms and draw sharp boundaries, which to Tor is also linked to being rebellious in the positive meaning of the term. His main motivators are therefore researchers who in some way or other challenge the field they are working within – among others, he especially highlights Albert North Whitehead, Bruno Latour, Karl Weick and Barbara Czarniawska.

Tor describes himself as 'a bit like Don Quixote; I think I sort of move ahead because I am impatient within my field'. To Tor, impatience is thus a personal trait that continuously leads him in new directions. But this trait also seems to mirror his interest in fluid mechanics as a young engineering student and what later became his main research focus: process and time.

3.   Looking at something

> A person who has no horizon does not see far enough and hence
> over-values what is nearest to him. On the other hand, 'to have a
> horizon' means not being limited to what is nearby but being able to see
> beyond it.
> (Hans-Georg Gadamer, 1975 [2013], p. 313)

The above quote from Hans-Georg Gadamer mirrors a characteristic
of all the contributors – namely, a wish to go beyond what is already
there and to challenge existing assumptions. Therefore, they are all
open to real-life phenomena and to what is going on in practice, be
that in society at large or in specific organizational settings. But what
triggers curiosity? That is, what seems, or becomes, interesting to
look at, research further, and produce new knowledge about?

All researchers have assumptions that inform and constrain the way
they think about organizations, which in turn shapes what they look
at and seek to understand. The reaction 'That's interesting' is often a
clue that previously taken-for-granted aspects and assumptions have
been brought to attention or called into question (Karl Weick, 2014,
p. 190). In line with this, John Alford (2008, p. 362) states that any
theory about what *should be* is based on assumptions about what *is*.
In this chapter, we use the interview data to explore how the research
idea and empirical focus that form the basis for theorizing emerge.

SETTING THE SCENE

To conduct organizational studies is to look at something that is a
real part of people's everyday lives and experiences. Moreover, as the
contributors mainly base their theorizing on qualitative studies and
stress the act of observing as crucial to understanding, it makes sense
to dive into what it means to give practice, or phenomena, precedence.
Thus, we will present a short introduction to *existential* phenomenol-

ogy as a philosophical stand, based on Martin Heidegger's influential work from 1927, *Being and Time.*

Phenomenology is a break with the idea that the *truth* of how the world is organized can be perceived through rational reasoning. Instead, phenomenology is concerned with practice and seeks understanding through the way we as humans are *in* the world. Thus, the divide between ontology and epistemology in phenomenology is not clear-cut because there is a circular aspect between conditions for being and the way we understand the world. With regard to realization, the world is therefore perceived as a concrete reality, which the researcher himself or herself is both a part of and constitutive for, since he or she is always already part of the reality to be realized (Jacob Rendtorff, 2014). Consequently, Martin Heidegger states that before theorizing we are first and foremost beings in the world (*Dasein*) – a condition he also refers to as being 'thrown into the world' (Martin Heidegger, 1927 [2010]; Tor Hernes, 2014).

Martin Heidegger's main point is that the ontology of being is neglected in a Cartesian understanding since the notion *Cogito ergo sum* is for Martin Heidegger the second stage of such ontology and not the starting point (Martin Heidegger, 1927 [2010], p. 23). Martin Heidegger's change in starting point from theoretical reflections to existence, or being, as essential denotes a focus on what phenomena do and not solely what they are. The focus on being and phenomena as referential relations becomes a focus on practice, because we can only relate to phenomena in what they do for or to us. In this way Martin Heidegger goes from nouns to verbs (e.g., a hammer can only be studied as it 'hammers' before us) because phenomena only make sense in the context in which they appear (Jacob Rendtorff, 2014).

The contextual aspect of understanding also relates to humans, as being depends on being *referred to* – implying that being is essentially social (Martin Heidegger, 1927 [2010], p. 86). Thus, what Martin Heidegger refers to as world, or worldliness, is defined as the *total referential context* making temporality a constitutive condition for being. Time is defined as 'within-timeness' (ibid., p. 225), implying that we are always in the world in relation to others and time. Subsequently, Martin Heidegger states the ontological proposition that humans are historical and that we are grounded in temporality, which in this sense makes the world 'subjective'. Martin Heidegger thus introduces a historical dimension in knowledge production, implying that all scientific reflection is contemporary. This is a crucial turn away from universal knowledge as the objective of theorizing. Life is instead understood as the sum of a series of experiences, happening in time, which is why to be grounded in temporality refers to our ability to maintain the self as itself through the ongoing changes of experiences (ibid., p. 356). Accordingly, the unit of analysis in phenomenological analysis is driven by a focus on the interplay between phenomena, structures and processes, and hence a wish to understand these structures of meaning, which constitute the social world of beings – a world that is inter-subjectively constituted and communicated (Martin Heidegger, 1927 [2010]; Jacob Rendtorff, 2014). This point will be applied to reveal the contributors' positions in relation to practice, the subject matter, and the wider historical times in which they have been or are doing research.

ORGANIZATIONAL STUDIES AS PRACTICE ORIENTED

The contributors have different stances on and approaches to practice. Some are primarily interested in developing knowledge that is useful for practitioners, whereas others are more concerned with contributing to the academic body of knowledge. However, the variations cannot be divided into the traditional distinction between application-oriented and conceptual studies since all contributors stress that their theorizing is informed by a genuine curiosity about organizations as real-world phenomena. Thus, even when conceptual research is undertaken, an orientation towards practice is present in the thinking.

Moreover, organizations are a pervasive part of everyday life, so by the time someone becomes a student or researcher of organizations he or she already has much experience in being part of organizations – kindergarten, primary school, high school, college, university, recreational organizations, the military, and so on. Students and researchers therefore come to the field with existing assumptions about what organizations are and how they are supposed to function. As such, organizational research is an inherently practice-oriented field, permeated with practical experiences and suppositions.

Thus, when it comes to organizational studies, Martin Heidegger's point – that we as researchers cannot step outside of and look objectively at the phenomenon we are trying to understand – seems particularly important. This notion helps us remember that we are already always a part of the reality under study; among other things, because researchers are already a part of a particular organization with its own rules, norms and values – namely, a university. Given that organizational researchers are so embedded in the very phenomenon that they are trying to understand, how is it possible to know what it is interesting and useful to create new knowledge about? Andrew Van de Ven's answer to that question is: 'First you have got to come up with the idea by abduction, a creative insight.'

THE EMERGENCE OF INTERESTING IDEAS

The interview data indicates that research ideas emerge due to something that one experiences and that stands out as interesting or strange because it does not correspond to what one expects. This in turn requires an alertness to both large and small divisions from the expected and an ability to put into words what is new or taken for granted.

For example, Edgar Schein emphasizes that serendipity has played a large role in which research themes and ideas he has chosen to pursue during his career. To exemplify, he relates how he and his fellow psychology students 'would say something and the other person would reflect it back to us with practically the same words and then we would all laugh. We did not have a clue that it would later become a primary therapeutic technique.' The story emphasizes that ideas can emerge in different settings, including in the classroom – and also that a playful approach with words in interactions might be the groundwork for new insights.

Andrew Van de Ven tells a somewhat similar story, but in his example the insight emerged within the frame of a predefined project. During his PhD, Andrew Van de Ven was doing neighbourhood block studies together with his supervisor to identify the needs of the locals. The purpose was to give the locals the possibility of voicing their concerns and problems and they had expected that people would use this opportunity without any hesitation. However, what actually happened was that after they had given the introduction and opened the floor for people to provide their input, 'nobody talked! So André Delbecq [the supervisor] said: "Go to the library and find out what is going on here. Why does nobody talk?"' The library work paid off by showing three things: that minorities typically are quiet in plenary sessions, that the term 'nominal groups', which refers to a group in name only, could be relevant (since the locals did not necessarily know and trust each other), and that individual brainstorming creates more ideas than collective brainstorming. Building on the practical experience that nobody talked and the three insights from the literature, the nominal group technique was developed. With this technique, they turned the experienced anomaly into a precondition – the nominal group technique starts the session with individual brainstorming before opening the floor for discussion of the ideas. In other words, the nominal group technique, which later became a leading brainstorming technique, was developed based on an abductive interplay between an unexpected experience, literature and new understandings.

Geert Hofstede does not refer to serendipity or unexpected insights as such. Instead, he describes how the main insights that formed the basis for his theory on cultural dimensions emerged slowly over a long time and while doing many different activities. He started his research with empirical studies of employee perceptions of their workplace. As Manager of Personnel Research for Europe at IBM he was responsible for first conducting interviews with employees in all the countries where IBM was located and then developing a survey questionnaire based on the insights from the interviews. In the process, Geert Hofstede argued that the aspects of importance to employees in one country should be part of the survey for all countries. He states: 'The surveys were not meant to compare the countries. They were just meant to find out how IBM was functioning in all these countries.' The work later became the foundation for a research finding that emerged when Geert Hofstede was teaching international classes to managers, namely that differences in their way of thinking corresponded to those from the survey. This gave him a hunch that something interesting was at play. It therefore made him dive into social anthropology, and when bringing in those new elements, 'I discovered that the interesting thing was not the difference between different individuals. It was the difference between the different countries.' This experience led to the focus on national cultural differences and hence on new research directions.

The examples presented above do to some extent refute the idea that *first* you have to find the research idea. Sometimes the research idea does emerge quickly, among other things because it is clear that something is not as expected. At other times it is through the gradual accumulation of numerous different types of surprises, insights and findings that it becomes clear how to frame and study the topic that one is trying to understand better.

THE RESEARCH IDEA: CHANCE OR CHOICE?

Edgar Schein's story is a story of playfulness and experimentation, Andrew Van de Ven's example is about experiencing an anomaly and solving it through abductive reasoning, and Geert Hofstede's is that of seeing connections across settings. However, the main point transcending the presented stories is that insights might occur when either not looking, or when looking at something else. Returning to the quote by Hans-Georg Gadamer at the beginning of the chapter, this means that the contributors do not favour or over-value their own ideas and assumptions. Instead, they expose themselves to what is in front them, pay attention to what stands out as funny, interesting, unexpected, strange, and so on – and that leads them towards novel trajectories.

Of course, there are also more deliberately chosen paths, defined projects, and methodologies that influence what becomes the research topic. However, when research is presented we seldom hear about the unanticipated and emerging aspects of what it might be interesting to know more about or understand better – not only for the people involved but also for a wider audience. Therefore, it remains relatively unexplored how researchers discover the research ideas that they then choose to investigate further.

DECIDING WHICH GAPS TO ADDRESS

The interplay between chance and choice and the importance of abductive reasoning where both practice and theory are at play for framing the research idea stand somewhat in contrast to the discursively constructed process of academic investigation.

The normal story goes as follows. As researchers we identify a knowledge gap in the literature, start researching to address this gap and finally come up with new insights that either add to the existing knowledge base or push a field forward. Andrew Van de Ven also explicitly questions this grand narrative of research by stating: 'I am interested in gaps, but I am interested in the gaps between a theory and a phenomenon. These are not necessarily gaps, but rather huge themes, which have not been addressed.'

In addition to Andrew Van de Ven's focus on the gap between the practice he observes and the literature, Karl Weick suggests another way to think about gap filling, namely as: 'rereading my own stuff and wanting to improve the grasp of the writing (e.g., too little attention to "Ecological Change" in 1979 and 1995 books)'.

The stories and points mentioned in the above paragraphs show that it is not necessarily trivial to find a research idea that is interesting. Yet, it is also clear that both *small, ordinary things*, such as discussions in a classroom, as well as *huge themes* and *extraordinary events*, such as Weick's research about disasters, can give rise to research ideas and findings that challenge existing practices, solutions and assumptions – and perhaps even the entire field. What stands out, however, is that in all examples the trigger for (further) research was to a smaller or larger extent informed by one or more practical experiences.

WHAT TO LOOK AT

Even though all the contributors are concerned with practice, they focus on different things. Andrew Van de Ven's starting point is to focus on people and their problems and to be willing to be surprised and to work actively with framing the research problem: 'Do not ever believe that you understand the problem adequately.' Edgar Schein's starting point is also people. He emphasizes that his interest in relationships, and what goes on between people, is key to understanding his research. He explains how the personal skill of being empathetic has opened doors to both people and research opportunities: 'I learned how to be helpful [to practitioners], which led to this whole sequence of writing books about process consultation.' Both Andrew Van de Ven and Edgar Schein look at people and problems in order to support them by finding solutions.

Another way of looking at organizations and organizational practices, both inside and outside academia, is to be curious about what people say and how they say it. Kenneth Gergen stresses that the approach of an anthropologist where the focus is on how people talk about the world – including the stories that people tell and the metaphors and expressions they use – can open up for new perspectives, understandings and forms of action.

Kenneth Gergen and Barbara Czarniawska share a focus on metaphors and their transformative and generative power. They see metaphors as central images that can expand understanding and action, because they go beyond existing assumptions and open up for new associations. As such, metaphors are both images of practice as it is and of practice as it could be – but illustrated in a way that is neither too abstract nor too precise. Or in Barbara Czarniawska's words: 'When metaphors die they will become concepts … Because metaphors are not metaphors when everybody takes for granted that these two things are connected – for a metaphor you must be brought to another place, but when you assume this is how it is, it is not moving you to any place.'

Language is also a part of David Boje's approach to practice and theorizing. He describes how this focus is interlinked with both his teaching experience and a personal trait of being verbally oriented before becoming an academic writer. Thus, to him, stories as a pedagogical practice turned into a lasting concern with storytelling – as a research topic, research method, and form of presentation.

The above examples show that a given research theme can be looked at in different ways, and that the choice of foci to some extent depends on personal interests, skills and preferences. The mentioned foci points include: *people, problems, solutions, relationships, the use of language, metaphors* and *stories*. These points all emphasize the precedence of practice.

LOOKING AS CONDITIONED BY HISTORICAL TIMES

An additional aspect that seems to inform what becomes the subject matter is historical times. Karl Weick refers to the nature of the 1960s when asked how his focus on organizing came about. Change as an overall topic, and more specifically the challenging of existing notions about organization, e.g., flux over stability, became the basis for his research on how organizations organize and hence his process perspective. Partly related, Kenneth Gergen, Edgar Schein and Barbara Czarniawska tell how they as young scholars were part of a time where universities played with combinations – and where business and economy studies started to look towards other disciplines. In particular, the triangular combination of anthropology, psychology and sociology lay the ground for organizational studies to appear in the 1960s – a combination, or disciplinary melting pot, which opened up new research streams to the contributors, as anthropological methods and notions of culture and the grand theories of sociology, like systems theory, supplemented their schooling in social psychology.

On a more general level, one way or another, most contributors have been affected by living in what Eric Hobsbawm (1994) refers to as the 'age of extremes', that is, a century of profound changes and war. Many contributors were young during some of the major transformations and challenges in the twentieth century: World War II, the Korean War, the Vietnam War, the Iron Curtain of the Cold War and a break with existing family, identity and gender structures. Especially for young men, the issue of being drafted into the military influenced the choice of career and academic subject matter. For example, during his time in Vietnam as part of the US army, David Boje discovered that it was possible to get out of the army four months earlier than planned if he was going to college. Thus, he became the first one in his family to go to college and afterwards to be offered a university scholarship. Based on the same logic, Geert Hofstede decided to go to university before the age of 20 so he would not be conscripted to Indonesia as a soldier. Later he served two years of military service in the Netherlands. There is not necessarily a causal link between this part of history and what the contributors came to look at as researchers. However, being raised during World War II, being enrolled in the Korean War or the Vietnam War, or being affected by political restrictions shaped either the conditions for working as an academic or what became individual interests and concerns.

In Box 3.1, Edgar Schein tells a story of how being enrolled in the Korean War turned into a research opportunity.

BOX 3.1   TURNING A SITUATION INTO A RESEARCH OPPORTUNITY

Edgar Schein's story: 'For example, when I was in the military, I did not expect to be sent to Korea to interview prisoners of war who were returning from the Korean War. That was dumped in my lap, but I was a social psychologist interested in influence. I had been trained as that. So, the inspiration was to see that here I had an opportunity to look at a real case, not an academic case, of how we influence someone. These people had been indoctrinated and I had an opportunity handed to me to study them. I was supposed to fly to Korea and get on a ship with several hundreds of these repatriates with a team to interview, diagnose and give whatever help they needed. My ship was delayed for three weeks, so I was sitting in Inchon with nothing to do … I decided to set up shop and start interviewing repatriates as they were coming off the trucks. I would randomly pick people and say: "Tell me your story. From the moment, you were captured what happened to you?" That became my first major paper called "The Chinese indoctrination program for prisoners of war" [1956] … I would call that being very cleverly adaptive. I think that has always been my strength: to turn whatever is around and what is going on around me into something analytically and practically useful.'

How history is influencing current research can only be understood in hindsight, hence we cannot say what in retrospect will be considered the main frame of reference for current academic knowledge production. However, from the vantage point of the present, there seems to be at least two major trends.

First, *specialization* rather than combination. Whereas the 1960s to the 2000s saw the emergence of many combination studies and cross-disciplinary research was considered beneficial, the trend today seems to be towards specialization. For example, in Denmark, many university programmes that combined philosophy and business, humanities and technology, and so on, were developed in the 1990s and 2000s. Now, however, there is governmental pressure to reduce the number of university studies on offer and for recommending studies that are clearly focused on maths, economics, organization, and so forth. Prospective students have listened to this and combination studies seem to be less in demand. Similarly, the increasing number of publications within all research fields seems to demand more specialization, as keeping up with the goings-on and published knowledge in one's field is a demanding task. As Karl Weick reflects in the interview: 'I grew up [in a time] with … less fragmentation of topics into more specialities.' Andrew Van de Ven likewise states that, 'there is more and more accumulation of literature and it is impossible to read it all, so you have to be more focused on a specific domain'.

Second, somewhat contradictory to the increased focus on specialization, another major theme is larger *societal challenges* such as climate change, increase in population, and flow of refugees, that is, issues that need to be addressed as shared challenges. These themes are already setting the agenda across research disciplines, illustrated by concepts such as sustainability, social economy and innovation.

The above reminds us that we are in the world at a specific period in time, implicating that as both humans and researchers we are reflected in the wider context of history, or, in Martin Heidegger's terms, in the *total referential context* of being. This underscores how academic knowledge production is deeply embedded in history – both with regard to research topics but also with regard to ways of doing research.

In Box 3.2, Andrew Van de Ven gives his account of how the research agenda in the social science field has changed *over* time and *with* historical times.

BOX 3.2   CHANGING RESEARCH AGENDAS

Andrew Van de Ven states: '[The] social science field has developed some norms over the years about how to address important questions. It started for me in the field of behaviourism – you observe what people do, you observe what organizations do and if you are going to be a good scientist you simply describe that. By doing that you can answer a number of interesting behavioural questions. Way back in the 1970s came the cognitive terms, Karl Weick and sensemaking, all focusing on cognition. Now when you start thinking of cognitive ways of thinking, good rational and irrational thinking, you can answer another set of questions that behavioural theory never could. Along the way, maybe in the 1990s, came the emotional terms. Emotion, passion, love and hate are things that cognition cannot explain, nor behaviour. It helps us understand the human condition better and now what do we know? It is clear that at least faith, religion, religiosity can address a whole host of questions that behaviour, cognition and emotion cannot. Why do people go to church on Sunday? The answer is because they are searching for meaning. A meaning in life that is not explained by our social science today, but fortunately the field of religiosity and spirituality in management has been flourishing in the past years into some real insight on how good, respectable social science can study and understand conditions where people are vulnerable.'

WAYS OF LOOKING

Now that we have related how historical circumstances shape the research conditions and interests, another topic arises – that focusing on *what* to look at implies a focus on *how* to look.

Most contributors are based in qualitative research, for some due to schooling and for others simply because it seems the most intuitive way to approach the phenomenon under study. To exemplify, despite Geert Hofstede's application of surveys in his studies of cultural differences he maintains that this needs to be reflected in practice. Therefore, talking to people to validate and discuss the statistical findings is key. He says: 'I also wanted to have an audience to discuss my findings with; experienced managers from different companies that could teach me as much as I could teach them.'

Edgar Schein started out as a dedicated experimentalist, doing controlled tests, but, in pace with work opportunities where he got to meet new inspirational senior researchers, he turned towards studies in real-life settings. He says: 'McGregor [Douglas McGregor, 1960 [2006]] was a psychologist writing about the human side of enterprise. I became his student and adopted his philosophy: that the important thing is your attitude and assumptions about people. Do you have faith in people or do you think about them cynically? He became my major source of conceptual influence.'

The above examples highlight the importance of academic team work. To look is basically also to look with others. Most contributors relate how as either junior researchers they have been invited into existing research or as seniors have been, or are, the ones to cultivate collaboration. In this sense, looking with somebody can both guide the research topic and the research approach – which in both cases is perceived as a way to become better and to understand deeper. As Andrew Van de Ven underscores: 'Don't fall in the trap of seeing the same people, the same students, in the same faculty every day. Try to go out and study the field for opportunities. Just observe and watch.'

In general, Andrew Van de Ven's research approach is to be profoundly engaged *in* practice *with* practitioners. He underscores this:

> For me what is productive and impactful is phenomenon-driven studies, where you kick yourself out of your office and get into the field, talk to people and find out and listen carefully to the problems they have. What are their issues and what are their concerns? And if we can apply our research and knowledge to those issues then we can have not only impact, but also get a variety of experiences.

To sum up, ways of looking are to a large extent about one's assumptions about and approach to people, both people who are a part of the phenomenon under study (research informants and participants) and people who are more detached and able to discuss whether the research findings seem plausible.

EMPIRICAL DATA

Organizational research often involves empirical data. We normally refer to empirical data as if we all know what this means, but, interestingly, among the contributors there are quite different perceptions of what data *is* and how to use it.

Perhaps the most common way is to think of data as empirical data (including both primary and secondary as well as quantitative and qualitative data) that is collected to address a particular research theme or question. However, as pointed out throughout this chapter, experiences and observations made over time from living, working, being part of research projects, and so on, create a storehouse of assumptions, expectations, stories, anecdotes, hunches and guesses. These can also be seen as data that influences one's thinking and that can be put to more or less articulated use – for making comparisons, connections, associations and generalizations – during theorizing. As Karl Weick states: 'Use your own living as your best data site (it won't mess you up).'

USING EMPIRICAL DATA

When it comes to using data, one view is that empirical data is both the starting point for and the main driver of the theorizing process. Edgar Schein is an advocate of this approach. He explains: 'You start with good observations, field work and interviews and draw theory out of that.' Thus, for Edgar Schein, theorizing is to make a lot of observations and to begin to see patterns in the data.

However, there are pitfalls associated with a data-driven approach to theorizing. Thus, it can create a more or less justified fear that there will be nothing of interest in the data, and that you therefore will have nothing to say. Barbara Czarniawska says that she understand people's anxiety. 'They are reading their field notes, and thinking: "What if I don't associate with anything? What if I don't find anything?" This is normal.' And sometimes the fear is justified and no pattern *can* be discerned, even when an enormous effort was put into systematically collecting a large amount of data. For example, Edgar Schein describes that he designed a longitudinal research study to collect qualitative and quantitative data about how people are influenced by the companies they work for and how this effects their careers:

[A]nd then I had the experience that all researchers have: I do not see any patterns. Some people moved toward their company, a lot of people left the company before I had any data, some people moved in the opposite direction from the company. Having invested all this effort, I had very little to show for it, except a lot of data about how random the corporate career is. How many switches people make. How varied companies are. It was very difficult to see patterns.

Another point is that, even with a data-driven approach to theorizing, data can primarily provide an interesting, revealing context for thinking (Henry Mintzberg, 2005). This view suggests that empirical data is a stepping stone for allowing the mind to roam freely and creatively as it is by musing like mad that theory can be developed. Thus: 'No generalizing beyond the data, no theory. And no theory, no insight. And if no insight, why do research?' (ibid., p. 10).

As such, empirical data can be seen as an important starting point and trigger for the theorizing process, but whether or not it is the main driver for the research depends on the type of research as well as on personal preferences and skills. In line with this, Tor Hernes sees himself as a conceptual writer, but without going into practice there would be less inspiration and less to conceptualize upon. He states: 'I am inspired by practice. One of the happiest moments are talking to people, recording data.' He further relates that while this is the case, when he tries to write empirical pieces they are not as easy for him to publish as his conceptual writing is.

Another view on the use of data is that it plays a more peripheral role, as the main point is to say what you want to say as well as you can possibly say it. With this perspective on theorizing, you do not need to have a thousand proven data points before you are allowed to say something. Instead, data serves as illustrations. Kenneth Gergen states:

> According to constructionism, empirical data is just like illustrations. They do not prove anything. They are just what you need to make something alive, vivid or powerful. My wife and I do a lot of work on what we call positive ageing ... We will use data that will show that if you have a negative view on ageing at the age of 60, your lifespan will be seven years less than if you are positive about it. It is powerful data. Of course, you can go on forever questioning what was the sample size, the statistics, what were the selectivity, and so on, but as an illustration of the possibility it is really powerful. So, I use data as illustrations and not as proof.

Based on the above there seems to be (at least) three positions towards the use of empirical data: a position where empirical data is the *main driver* for theorizing throughout the process; a middle ground where empirical data is considered a useful *starting point* for theorizing beyond the data; and a position where empirical data is primarily used *after* theorizing to make the theoretical points come alive.

SUMMARY

This chapter has emphasized that being open to phenomena in front of you and to have a horizon are the basis for seeing beyond what is already (out) there but also beyond one's own knowledge base. The data material reveals many stories of discovering new issues while looking at something else or in another direction, that is, looking at something and then realizing that a slight change opens up for new ideas and appearances. It is also evident that this openness towards displacements is driven by a personal trait of curiosity alongside an urge to understand either a problem or a challenge in a real-life setting and subsequently make this the foundation for research. Tor Hernes's advice is to:

> [s]earch for a phenomenon, a phenomenon that combines an empirical setting and a set of concepts. For example, apply trust to religion ... and then do profound empirical research based on that. It is a way to get a setting and really go a long way with a few selected ideas. (Tor Hernes)

As mentioned at the beginning of the chapter, it seems that the contributors' profound preoccupation with understanding both empirical and theoretical matters somehow erases the distinction between conceptual and application-oriented studies, first because they all are concerned with practice and furthermore because no one wants to do research that is not put into play outside academia – one way or the other. In this manner, they not only look into problem and issues, they are also highly solution oriented. Thus, for the contributors to be directed towards something and the issues that this direction informs can be understood as *potential* food for thought. This means that the process of theorizing begins or evolves around a topic that seems relevant enough to be looked into in the first place. As has become clear, there might be different triggers for pursuing an idea or insight further or taking on a societal challenge, but basically it narrows down to the question – what calls for thinking (Martin Heidegger, 1968 [2004])?

BOX C   GEERT HOFSTEDE – THE PERSONAL NARRATIVE

Geert was born in 1928 in the Netherlands. At that time the second language was French, but due to the German occupation during World War II it changed to German, and subsequently English became a key language in Holland. Among other things because of this, Geert is a gifted linguist and perceives that his linguistic skills have framed his research interests and his ability to get inspiration from many sources – both because of easy access to ideas written in different languages and through relationships.

World War II also framed what was possible for the young Geert to do. The universities were a mess and hence his father recommended that he attended a technical college instead, which meant that at age 18 he did internships in Dutch companies for a year. This led him to the Dutch East India Company, where he noticed the tensions between the Indonesian independence movement and the Dutch government, but mostly he was just thrilled to see more of the world. After his return from Asia, the government decided that young men wanting to attend university should do so before the age of 20, otherwise they would be send to Indonesia as soldiers. Thus, Geert graduated from Delft Technical University in 1953 with an MSc in mechanical engineering and then did his military service in the Netherlands. Afterwards, he worked some years in industry and then in the 1960s the education law was changed, giving him the opportunity to do a PhD in a programme other than his master's. Consequently, Geert became the first mechanical engineer in Holland to obtain a PhD degree in social psychology.

Geert has primarily worked as a practitioner but since 1971 he has been affiliated on and off to academic institutions. His main research interest is national cultural differences, first prompted by employee surveys at IBM and then refined when employed at INSEAD and the European Institute for Advanced Studies in Management. Throughout his work life it has been important to him to have a clear understanding of the people he addresses – from his work as a factory worker as a newly graduated engineer to his focus on employees as manager and consultant. His academic career is in this setting unusual as he only became a university professor eight years before he retired (from 1985 to 1993) – a period he refers to as one of the unhappiest of his work life, due to what he experienced as bickering among ambitious people uninterested in the practical application of their work. Geert has been married to Maaike for 62 years and is, in his own words, blessed with four sons, ten grandchildren and three great-grandchildren.

Behind the scenes – interviewing Karl Weick

> The essential human act at the heart of writing is the act of giving.
> (Peter Elbow, 1998, p. 20)

Karl Weick preferred to contribute in writing and he therefore answered our interview question guide (see the Appendix to this book) with some deeply considered comments. To acknowledge Karl Weick's generosity and thoroughness and to engage in dialogue, first Anne wrote personal thoughts and comments and subsequently Sabine replied to both Karl and Anne. The interview was then sent back to Karl.

Returning to the interview in the analysis phase, we once again found it both inspiring and readable. Together with Karl Weick we therefore agreed to present the interview, with our comments, in full below. The aim is both to provide the reader with the treat of Karl Weick's replies and to give a glimpse behind the scenes of making this book. This is achieved in the following ways:

- The general questions in the interview question guide are the same as in the verbal interviews conducted with the other contributors. In the interview question guide we invited the contributors, and in this case, Karl Weick, to think about their personal approach to theory and theorizing.
- Karl Weick's written response provided insight into the act of expressing thought and how meaning is created through writing. This is apparent throughout the interview as a whole not only because it is a *written* interview; it is also apparent in Karl Weick's statements *about* writing. He emphasizes that one of his key theorizing practices is to write in order to develop insights (backstage writing for the purpose of clarifying his own thinking) and then to think of these pieces

of writing and insights as a mosaic that can be assembled into a whole that is meaningful to others (frontstage presentation to an audience).

• After Karl Weick had completed the interview, we read it and could not help but make personal comments triggered by his text – with regard to what it meant to each of us as well as in the context of this book.

Finally, at the copy-editing stage, for the sake of completeness and to direct the reader to further reading, citations of some of Karl Weick's and other authors' works were inserted in square brackets where we were certain which work Karl was referring to.

This chapter therefore provides insight into the dialogical nature of how reading, writing and thinking occurs in practice. In this way, the chapter *shows* (rather than describes) how new thoughts and understanding emerge through a social and sharing-oriented process.

THE INTERVIEW

The Personal Narrative

What was your background for entering academia?

Karl: My 'background' is not obviously relevant. Before undergrad and grad school I was basically a late-night disc jockey on radio. That world consists of talking, independence, orchestrating moods, telling stories, improvising, all of which can play some part in academia. But radio looked like a dead-end career. I was honestly without any idea of what I wanted to be when I started undergraduate school. I continued to do radio shows part-time while an undergraduate. My grades weren't great. I didn't so much 'enter' academia as 'stumble' into it when I saw the kind of work that superb faculty members did and wanted to be able to do the same things some day.

Anne: I like the idea of stumbling – it seems in general closer to reality than *entering* a domain, a relationship, a position, and so on.

What influenced your decision to have an academic career?

Karl: Terrific undergraduate professors at Wittenberg University (Remsberg, Rahn, Roselius, Nave, Dudycha, Coyle). My good fortune continued in graduate school at Ohio State University where I worked with the fabulous professor, Harold B. Pepinsky. I loved psychology and couldn't think of a better way to remain in touch with it than to study and teach it.

Anne: This underscores an assumption of the book – that it is both about the people that one meets and works with, and the profession itself.

Thinking back, what have been/are the most thrilling things about being in academia?

Karl: Not sure 'thrilling' is the way I would describe being in academia. Being in academia is stimulating, animating, enlivening, and moving. What this boils down to is that academia fosters and often rewards continuing curiosity. And the emphasis is on 'continuing' as much as on curiosity itself. Academia is a 24/7 immersion, and has been this way long before '24/7' became a fashionable contemporary phrase to feign engagement. Mundane thrills in academia include getting paid to study, continuous discussion, smart colleagues, no boss, inquiring as the work, and ongoing connecting with people and ideas. I love being an academic! As an important footnote, my enthusiasm is largely influenced by experiences from 1958 to 2012. The academia on which I reflect is sometimes tough to spot in today's academic life.

Anne: I will be happy if this book can make junior researchers go with their curiosity and engagement, and not only with what is strategically convenient and/or necessary for job security.

Inspiration

Under what circumstances do you feel most inspired?

Karl: If I could answer this, I could increase the number of times I *do* feel inspired. Components include a high level of energy; a quotation that cries out to be glossed at length; rereading something of my own that is as good as I can do and thinking, 'I'm ready to do that again'; a deadline and an outlet that I value highly; an invitation to contribute that has an intriguing twist; a routine that becomes associated with the production of a spurt of connected ideas (e.g., first two hours of every day are pure gold for thinking that gets refined the rest of the day).

Do you deliberately seek inspiration? Where? How?

Karl: I certainly do seek inspiration deliberately but often fail to find it. And when I do find it, the sources are incredibly diverse. Inspiration has come from listening to big band jazz (e.g., Bill Holman's arrangement of 'Stompin at the Savoy'); browsing a magazine (e.g., 'Navy Commander hates frozen pizza and thinks it demoralizes his crew', found in naval *Proceedings Magazine*); rereading my own stuff and wanting to improve the grasp of the writing (e.g., too little attention to 'Ecological Change' in 1979 and 1995 books); spending a half-hour reading superb writing (e.g., William James's *Some Problems of Philosophy*), studying large photographs to detect a mood, missed details, and the effort made to create the scene (e.g., O. Winston Link's night-time photos of Norfolk & Western Railroad); studying entries in a dictionary of synonyms to see subtle differences between seemingly similar labels (e.g., *Merriam-Webster's Dictionary of Synonyms*); free associating with a pad and pencil to see what I say and might want to think about more deeply; copy great writing for a half-hour in order to get a feel for its rhythms and flow of ideas; and, like everyone else, sit and stare out the window, and try to accept that, just for today, inspiration is on vacation.

Anne: I think this answer highlights the usefulness of getting to know one's own inspirational triggers: settings, mode, literature, music, and so on, as well as accepting that inspiration cannot be pushed forward too hard.

Can you pinpoint a text (can be everything from a novel, an article, lyrics, poetry etc.) that has been especially inspirational to you?

Karl: Reinhold Niebuhr's 'Serenity Prayer'.

Anne: It makes me interested …

Have there been different inspirational texts at different points in your life/career?

Karl: It seems as if when I shifted from one university to another, my inspirational texts also changed. For example, at Purdue the 'inspirational text' was Leon Festinger's book on cognitive dissonance; at Minnesota it was Donald Campbell's work on socio-evolution; at Cornell it was Gregory Bateson's *Steps to an Ecology of Mind*; at the University of Texas it was Charles Perrow's *Normal Accidents*; and, at Michigan it has been John Dewey's *Human Nature and Conduct*, Emery Roe and Paul Schulman's *High Reliability Management*, and William James's collected writings.

Anne: You make me want to read all of the mentioned texts! I have also been very inspired by Gregory Bateson's *Steps to an Ecology of Mind*.

What texts/articles do you perceive as the canonical texts of your field?

Karl: Chester Barnard's *The Functions of the Executive*; James March and Herbert Simon's *Organizations*; Daniel Katz and Robert Kahn, *The Social Psychology of Organizations*; Walter Buckley, *Sociology and Modern Systems Theory*; Charles Perrow's *Normal Accidents*; Diane Vaughan, *The Challenger Launch Decision*; William H. Starbuck and Moshe Farjoun's *Organization at the Limit: Lessons from the Columbia Disaster*.

Anne: Thanks!

Which role have they played for you (as thought-provoking, inspiration, used to legitimize own writing)?

Karl: They are thought-provoking. But more than that, there is a sense that 'it is all there' about organizations and organizing. They convey this completeness only if you read each book slowly and appreciatively while paying close attention to the ways in which flow, sequence and patterning are captured by language that does justice to complexity.

Anne: Very good point on the time aspect – that the text, if read slowly, kind of unfolds. And also we can integrate the perception that

you share with the other contributors, that going back to the heritage
of the field is still extremely relevant and giving.

Can you reflect upon how a text becomes a canon text?

Karl: I just don't think in terms of texts that become or comprise
the canon. I suspect that what happens more often is that a text
becomes part of one's *personal* canon when it becomes a continuing
source of energy, ideas, connections, and literally yields 'gems' no
matter where it is opened. Canonical status can occasionally occur
surreptitiously when what one reads fuses with what one takes to be
one's own thoughts. Untangling the fusion and accurately attribut-
ing credit can be difficult. I think this is why we favour images such
as 'standing on the shoulders of giants', it's all been said before,
scholarship is cumulative, and knowledge is collective omniscience.
I know it's a truism but in matters relating to the canon, authors
can control inputs but not outcomes. Canonical texts are overde-
termined. I'm more comfortable hearing about 'a' canon than 'the'
canon.

Anne: Good point – we will take this into account!

Theorizing

*We apply the term 'to theorize' – is this meaningful to you (which term
would you prefer)? Or what do you understand by theory?*

Karl: I like the term 'inquiry' as much as I like the term 'theorizing'. John Dewey favoured the term inquiry: 'In Dewey's approach
to inquiry there is no sharp boundary between everyday life and
research. Instead, research is simply a form of inquiry that is
performed more carefully and more self-consciously than most
other responses to problematic situations … [I]nquiry is just one
form of experience, and research is just one form of inquiry' (David
L. Morgan, 2014, 'Pragmatism as a paradigm for social research',
Qualitative Inquiry, **20**(8), 1045–53; quotation is on page 1047). As
for 'theorizing', I think the 'object' and 'goals' of this activity are
more varied than people realize. Philip and Margaret Runkel (1984,
p. 130) make this point: 'Theory belongs to the family of words that
includes guess, speculation, supposition, conjecture, proposition,

hypothesis, conception, explanation, model. The dictionaries permit us to use theory for anything from "guess" to a system of assumptions ... [Social scientists] will naturally want to underpin their theories with more empirical data than they need for a speculation. They will naturally want a theory to incorporate more than one hypothesis. We plead only that they do not save theory to label their ultimate triumph, but use it as well to label their interim struggles.' Theorizing as interim, ongoing struggles to flesh out hunches feels about right.

Anne: You open up the concept to me, thanks. Also I always related inquiry to natural sciences, so now I might start applying it a bit more.

Sabine: For me, it is useful to think about the *process* of theorizing. When thinking about it as a process, it becomes more apparent and acceptable for me as a quite result-oriented person that it takes time, patience and effort to get to the results – and that the process is important and delightful in itself (at least some of it/to some extent). However, I think I would use the term 'to conceptualize' to express what it is I actually do during the process of theorizing. That is, during the process of theorizing I conceptualize the topic I am studying by experimenting with figures, tables, labels, names and metaphors to see if they fit. When the concepts seem to fit, it is (1) because they highlight the important differences and similarities (patterns) and foregrounds the unique aspects of (my own and/or others') experiences with the topic under study. And (2) because they make sense to others too, and not just to me.

How would you characterize your process of theorizing/theory building (structured/unstructured, creative/analytical)?

Karl: My process is akin to constructing a mosaic. Parts, paragraphs, phrases, mini-essays are gathered and moved around until something resembling a pattern seems to exist. The pattern is given a name. Thus, theorizing is assembling, fitting, and seeing patterns in an assemblage, although, like mosaics, there are gaps between parts. That is why this process is not quite what Ernest Boyer has called 'the scholarship of integration'. Holistic views of the assemblage are sometimes hard to envision because of these gaps. But sometimes those gaps get filled by means of mechanisms that link macro to micro (situational mechanisms), micro to micro (action formation mechanisms), or micro to macro (transformational mechanisms). The process I have described is basically what William Shakespeare described in *A Midsummer Night's Dream* (Act V, Scene I), when Theseus says that poets imagine 'airy nothing' into hunches about forms and shapes unknown, which are then pinned down to a local habitation and given a name. The Theseus sequence (airy nothing > imagination > forms > shapes > local habitation > a name) is one way to do theorizing. At each step there is editing, but what is being edited is the *concreteness* of unconceptualized experience ('airy nothing'). The products of that editing are abstractions that seem to be concrete because they have a location and a name. But that habitation and its name are merely abstract substitutes for the manyness of less conceptualized experience ('airy nothing').

Anne: This is beautiful – and to me it stresses the importance of going with a hunch, even when you cannot see the full range of the argument yet.

Sabine: This makes me think of a statement that (I think) is attributed to W.H. Auden: 'Poetry is the clear expression of mixed feelings.' With a slight rewriting to fit academia – and inspired by your distinction between unconceptualized and conceptualized experiences – it could be: 'Research (in the social sciences/organizational studies) is the clear expression of ambiguous experiences.'

What/who supports your thinking?

Karl: Co-authors such as, in my case, Kathleen Sutcliffe keep the thinking going and this leads to refining. Support means keeping the thought unfolding so that more associations and better language have time to develop. Encouragement is certainly supportive, as are routines of thinking (e.g., when you read, write in the margins).

Anne: Again time is a key aspect – and encouragement, which is the main aim of the book. Also, we have started to discuss that across interview answers there is an inherent critique of the way academia is developing, including the conditions for being an academic.

What can be a barrier to your thinking process?

Karl: Concerns about the reception of the work; noise; low mood; social comparison; no one to discuss ideas with; absence of a riveting example; inability to visualize an audience; distractions of surfing the web; reminiscence.

Anne: This is very honest and very important – and we have seen the same in other interviews. I would very much like to pass on the insight that these thinking processes have an element of anxiety also for seniors and giants.

Sabine: Yes, and it seems that there are different types of anxiety at play: The 'am I good enough and is what I am doing worthwhile' type (existential angst), the 'am I able to express all the thoughts I have in my head so that they are intelligible to others' type, the 'am I able to produce something that is good enough fast enough' type (performance anxiety), and the fear of how others will react to the work (reception anxiety). To some extent, it is a comfort to know that others, including already well-established seniors, feel the same; but of course, it also means that there is then no reason to assume that the anxiety will disappear later in life.

Looking at your own work, what are the relations between theorizing and the analytical concepts that you have developed?

Karl: For want of a better depiction, it seems like concepts are sometimes simply declared when one is otherwise preoccupied with answering the question, 'What's the story?' Concepts also can emerge when I work backwards from a phrase and ask what it might involve, how it might vary, and what role context would play. For example, I have mixed feelings toward the concept of 'balance' and have said so in different places. But I am intrigued by D.H. Lawrence's phrase, 'the trembling balance'. That phrase has an uncertainty, an animation, a precariousness that, when developed, might well enable one to rework processes such as managing the unexpected.

Anne: Being concerned with language, I like the point that concepts are contextual and come with different underpinnings – and that we can play with them by adding new words or applying them in new ways.

Sabine: I have recently published a Danish book entitled *Understanding Change – The Balance Between Process and Results* (translation) together with a co-author [Anita Mac and Sabine Madsen, 2017]. We were never happy with the title, because it somehow suggests that it is possible to find the 'right' balance if only one is well-educated/clever/professional/understanding enough. The distinction between process and results is a useful abstraction, for analytical and planning purposes. However, everyday life quickly shows that most of the time the two are mixed together when we speak, act and try to accomplish whatever it is we wish to accomplish. That is, process and results are intertwined and you cannot have one without the other, but at given points in time you can focus more on one than the other. The trembling balance sounds like a great metaphor to capture this – as (Google says): the trembling balance refers to *the dynamic experience of life's quickness* and necessarily involves giving up the quest for static equilibrium. To me, trembling also suggests something that can both mean to quiver with anxiety and to vibrate with energy, which also seems to capture the mixed feelings and ambiguous experiences connected with change. Thank you very much for this metaphor.

How did the focus on organizing rather than organization come about? And how is it related to your application of loose coupling?

Karl: A partial answer to the question of 'focus' is the nature of the 1960s (the first edition of [*The Social Psychology of*] *Organizing* was written during the 1960s and published in 1969). 1969 is the year we landed on the moon (20 July) and the same year that the infamous guns-on-campus episode happened at Cornell University (20 April). During the 1960s, protests against the Vietnam War were sites where organizing occurred, existing organizations were attacked, change was the predominant topic, and flux rather than stasis was common-place. Forming and dissolving were more common than stability. In addition, my own work was mainly process oriented, such as, for example, investigation of the ways in which orchestras became more organized during rehearsals; ways in which information overload was managed by a series of strategies conceptualized by James G. Miller;

laboratory tasks that stretched across generations (e.g., Karl Weick and David Gilfillan, 1971); and efforts to create a processual supplement to Daniel Katz and Robert Kahn's important work on the social psychology of organizations. The emerging languages of social evolution, emergence, and systems theory also primed attention to organizing. Closer examination of systems suggested that interdependencies unfolded at different rates of speed with different degrees of determinacy among steps. Those variations in determinacy were gathered together under the label 'loose coupling', a label that was already evident in work by [James G.] March, and [John W.] Meyer and [Brian] Rowan.

Anne: A nice note here is that academia is always also deeply embedded in and reflective of a historical context.

Sabine: Yes, the theoretical ideas and concepts that become popular seem to emerge as a response to what is happening in society (i.e., conceptualizing as a game of catch-up), at the same time as they work back on and shape society (i.e., conceptualizing as world-making). This puts emphasis on the history of ideas.

How did the concept of sensemaking emerge?

Karl: The concept developed in part from my early interest in existentialism (e.g., Camus's statement that philosophy's 'one serious problem is suicide': William James's assertion that you can answer the question, 'Is life worth living?' with either a yes or no and then enact the truth of the answer). The concept was also stirred by discussions with Harold Garfinkel regarding accounts, indexicals, and retrospect, coupled with my research on action as a means to reduce post-decision contradictions. People seem to have a stake in their justifications and try to shape the world to fit them. If they are partially successful in this fitting then they are better able to manage anxiety. One implication is that anxiety reduction through self-justification may help hold one's world together. Organizational culture is often defined in terms of acceptable justifications. This is a different twist on 'organizational fit' since it suggests that people in need of support for their justifications are more likely to find that support in some settings but not in others. A meshing of justifications would amount to a good fit.

Anne: I now feel wiser! And I also feel like a little girl happy to realize that a master has had the same interest as myself – as a teen I was deeply concerned with existentialism, reading Camus, Sartre and de Beauvoir. The perception of absurdity as a precondition is still part of my mindset today.

What is it that making sense/sensemaking stresses as opposed to, for example, meaning making or organizational culture?

Karl: The process of sensemaking is focused on short-term, satisfactory (plausible), provisional understandings that enable a person or group to keep going and to engage in further actions that refine and update initial hunches. As one updates provisional understandings, this revising may engage deeper, more long-term experiences, in which case sensemaking blends into meaning making. This movement from sense to meaning is also reversible. Meanings collapse and sensemaking itself can become problematic. These transitions and what they reveal have been a significant window for me on sensemaking. Precursors of disasters (e.g., Mann Gulch, Bhopal, Tenerife airport), their unfolding, and post-hoc examination of them, suggest concepts that relate to sensemaking under extreme conditions (e.g., cosmology episode). But, it is an act of faith on my part that I think similar conditions scale down to less extreme occasions.

Anne: Very interesting and enlightening. I have been working on a project regarding fire safety in the maritime sector and I agree – the actions/reactions in extreme situations mirror the assumptions and understandings enacted in daily practices.

How did you approach existing literature within your field? And which role did the existing literature play with regard to the formulation of the concept of sensemaking (inspiration, criticism of the existing literature, positioning)?

Karl: I draw very wide boundaries around what constitutes the 'existing' literature, clear up to the point where that literature can occasionally mean whatever 'exists' at the top of my 'To Read' stack. When my hand touches the top of the stack, *that's* the existing literature. Literature is absolutely central to everything I do, but sometimes in less common ways. For example, I sometimes read the literature and then write, but I'm just as likely to write in order to discover what I should read. I write a story. Could this have happened? I reach for writing by Gregory Bateson, computational theorists, the Stoics, Agnes Martin, or Lance Sandelands, all of whom may suggest answers. Built into this writing-in-search-of-reading is a strong temptation toward confirmation bias. That certainly does operate. And sometimes that operation can be motivational. 'Gee, I didn't realize that this idea made that much sense to so many people', except that those who thought the idea was foolish and absurd somehow went unnoticed. The antidote? A storehouse of varied reading and a comfort with free associating in search of items that are relevant, not just supportive.

Anne: I like the point of relevancy – and that boundaries are not fixed regarding a specific research domain.

What are you most proud of in your work?

Karl: The whole concept of 'proud' makes me uneasy. As I was growing up (b. 1936), to be proud was to be boastful, cocky, conceited, none of which were desirable. So, any kind of self-evaluation of my work as something in which I took pride was uncommon and worrisome when invoked. What then would serve as substitutes for pride? An indirect indication would be citations. In addition, substitutes take the form of qualities of works rather than the entire work itself. For example, I like the mixture of cartoons and science in the second edition of *Organizing* [1979]. The juxtaposition of serious with ironically serious is just the tone I like to capture. I like the applications of organizing and sensemaking that are the foundations of the three editions of *Managing the Unexpected* co-authored with Kathleen Sutcliffe [2001, 2007, 2015]. I like the thin compactness of the 1969 version of the *Organizing* book just as I like the thick wide-ranging quality of the *Sensemaking* book [Karl Weick, 1995b]. I like the summary quality of both my article on Transient Reliability (*Journal of Contingencies and Crisis Management* [Karl Weick, 2011]) and my 'Last Lecture' that I presented at Michigan in September 2012. Those 'likings' are as close to a feeling of pride as I am likely to get.

Anne: I would not like to apply the term proud either – but this has to do with me relating it to some individual achievement and I prefer to achieve something together with others. I would go for the term 'like' as you do!

Here comes a question on behalf of a lot of our students: are they allowed to challenge and contest your theory?

Karl: 'Allowed?' Who said they weren't allowed? Challenge and contesting are productive, but more so when everyone is mindful of the recipe: 'How can I know what I think until I see what I say?' If students pay attention to what they say, and I do the same, and both of us work to get a closer alignment between the saying and the thinking, then the learning is incredible. Academia is not a place for people with thin skins. But again, you've got to modify that observation to account for changes across time and context. Academia induces the thinning and the thickening of skin as circumstances change. Responses to contesting as well as the contesting itself are not constant. We all claim that we are always open to challenge and contesting. Occasionally we stumble when we walk that talk.

Anne: The 'allowed' aspect is based on our experience with students actually asking if they are allowed. We are as puzzled as you are.

Sabine: We had an email dialogue with James March and he kindly gave us one of his poems to include in our book. One of the lines in the poem is the following: 'Research is not for sissies.'

Academic Craftsmanship

We refer to you as a 'giant of organizational research'. This is based on the sentence 'to stand on the shoulders of giants' – what do you perceive by this?

Karl: I value the description (though not as a description of myself), but regret the fact that many don't take it seriously. As a result, they say many of the same things that the giants said earlier and regrettably, do so less clearly.

Anne: This might be a focal point in *Theorizing in Organization Studies: Insights from Key Thinkers*!

Being a junior researcher, how did you approach existing giants?

Karl: I read their work closely, corresponded with them (roughly 80 per cent replied), tried to learn how they worked by talking to their students and reading footnotes and attending their symposia, and tried to be respectful, deferential, and well-enough informed to sustain conversations with several of them. From the beginning I 'played the percentages', figuring that if I keep writing I can write my way into occasional insights. Long before I heard the phrase, my style was to see what I wrote in order to learn what I thought.

Anne: Very interesting to learn about your writing practice – and that you sometimes write forward the realization instead of the other way around.

Sabine: Both you and all the other contributors stress the importance of being able to build personal relationships with and/or correspond directly with existing giants, to get their honest feedback (and recognition), and through this, energy and confidence to keep working on an idea. My impression is that these correspondences are both valued much more and of far more importance in pushing the thinking forward than the anonymous review system – which, very interestingly, no one has mentioned as important at all!

What would your advice be to current junior researchers?

Karl: You may hear this from your other interviewees, but I'm hesitant to give 'advice' because my career feels idiosyncratic. It is idiosyncratic in the sense that my work occurred at very early stages of topics, which meant I could pretty much define boundaries within which I could make a contribution. It is also idiosyncratic in a dispositional sense. In 1978, Mitroff-Kilmann used MBTI (Myers-Briggs Type Indicator) profiles to distinguish styles of theorizing. My profile, INTJ (introversion, intuition, thinking, judgement) is described as a 'speculative theorist who deeply values broad-ranging novel ideas, and who does not demand that these ideas be tied down to "reality" in the sense of being verified by accepted theories or facts. Indeed the CT [conceptual theorist] often prefers to challenge known facts and ideas, if only for the sake of speculative argument.

Above all, the CT values the creation of novel conceptual possibilities, schemata, and hypotheses which allow us to revise, rethink, and challenge even the most firmly entrenched and accepted ideas' (Ian Mitroff and Ralph Kilmann, 1978, p. 55).

I am wary of 'giving advice' because the context in which I worked seems different from what exists now. I grew up with less competition for jobs or space in publications or tenure, less fragmentation of topics into more specialities, fewer sessions at conventions with greater attendance and time for discussion, fewer costs of doing fewer things of higher quality, and greater valuation of big ears and big eyes rather than big data. So what advice makes sense? Be really clear what you're getting yourself into, and be sure that your partner is equally clear. Spend time with ideas that are more than five years old. Cultivate congenial co-authors. Keep writing and revising and editing in order to think more clearly. Use your own living as your best data site (it won't mess you up).

Anne: I am ENFP [extraversion, intuition, feeling, perception]. I believe that your advice, despite your reluctance to do so, is great. Partly my motivation for this book project is based on the notion: cultivate congenial co-authors – Sabine is one such person!

Sabine: I am INTJ [introversion, intuition, thinking, judgement] and this might go some way in explaining why our collaboration works really well, Anne. I am inspired by the notion of spending time with an idea (and also ideas that are more than five years old!). For me this sounds like spending time with a person. In general, I think that it is useful to remember that there are real people behind even the most abstract of ideas and that spending time with their ideas therefore means connecting with traces of their consciousness for a while.

Does the idea of a giant make it difficult to challenge theory?

Karl: Isn't the answer to this lodged in the eye of the beholder? The presumption that a giant is 'difficult to challenge' encourages an avoidance of challenge, which supports the presumption.

Anne: I rest my case.

In general, there is a focus on identifying knowledge gaps in literature so we can come up with new *knowledge – what do you think of this 'newness' expectation?*

Karl: I'm all for gap-filling, but the existence of a gap does not mean that it has to be filled. The truism, there's nothing new under the sun, seems right more often than it is wrong. That undoubtedly is an artefact of my reading more older work than newer work. I don't recommend that as a tactic. But it works for me. People under-estimate how often older work contains insights that got simplified over time and, when reworked, are able to refresh the new. This is a similar process to the one Sir Frederic Bartlett (1932) observed as people communicated a complex Canadian folktale ('The War of the Ghosts') from person to person. The conventional replaced the unique.

Sabine: I have been part of a book club for several years, where we read books/texts that preferably are around 500–2000 years old (e.g., a lot of Greek drama). This confirms that there really is nothing new under the sun – politics, duty vs indulgence and work–life balance also posed problems back then.

Anne: I feel grateful – and happy that Sabine and I were cheeky enough to write to you.

4. Finding your academic family

There is no amount of things you cannot learn from reading.
(English teacher in the coming-of-age movie *Handsome Devil*, 2016)

In the previous chapter, we looked at the contributors' stories of how the research idea emerges and is shaped by the historical times as well as the individual researcher's assumptions, experiences and empirical observations of and insights about the phenomena under study. In this chapter, we use metaphors to try to understand which role the existing literature, and by extension the academic community, plays in theorizing.

The field of organizational studies is ripe with metaphors. The same can be said for the literature on philosophy of science, theory and theory development. One of the main metaphors connected with academic knowledge production is to 'stand on the shoulder of giants'. This saying is now so common that it has almost lost its original meaning and it is clear from our interviews that the statement has come to be associated with the publication game, career goals and incremental knowledge production. However, if we look at the statement from an inspirational point of view, it highlights the importance of knowing the people that came before you, the fathers and mothers of the field, and of finding your rightful place on those people's broad shoulders – if you are to find *your* historical roots and academic identity. This is both a matter of communal belonging and a personal matter of becoming yourself, as an academic and perhaps more generally as a human being.

In this chapter, we explore how people, places and publications influence the theorizing process. We draw on numerous concepts, metaphors and expressions to grasp this. However, we are particularly interested in developing the metaphor of 'an academic family' to incorporate and extend existing understandings of the literary and communal aspects of theorizing.

SETTING THE SCENE

Academic fields and communities are largely carried by the written word and a huge part of theorizing is to *draw on* the existing literature base. Therefore, it is relevant to know concepts and metaphors that can help shed light on what that actually means. To this end, we use the term 'intertextuality'. Intertextuality points out that any text is always based on and in dialogue with what already exists. As such, intertextuality questions how new and original any single text can ever be.

Julia Kristeva (1980) was the first to propose the term intertextuality. In line with the term itself, intertextuality was, of course, not new as such, but based on Ferdinand de Saussure's (1916 [2011]) focus on the individual text and its elements and Mikhail Bakhtin's theory about dialogism (Mikhail Bakhtin, 1981; Michael Holquist, 2003). The latter suggests that a text has a dialogical relationship with other texts and authors; a dialogue that does not stop but continues as new texts emerge.

If we look at the individual text first, intertextuality highlights that when a writer creates a text he or she draws on numerous elements such as genre conventions, direct quotes, references and more or less explicit allusions to other texts (Gérard Genette, 1997; Julia Kristeva, 1980). The use of these elements in turn allows the reader to decode the text, as both meaning (the main points of a paper) and layers of meaning (e.g., which authors and ideas are invoked through the use of some references and not others). This goes for all text, and it seems to be particularly true for academic texts. In general, the genre convention for academic publications requires that much extant knowledge is repeated in each paper – for example, in the literature review section, in the theory section and/or in the discussion section.

All this calls the idea of new knowledge production into question, at least with regard to the individual text and its ability to make an original contribution to the existing body of knowledge. Others (e.g., Nicolas Bourriaud, 2002) claim that while this might be true, the way the author(s) of a particular text weaves the already existing ideas and text chunks together always creates new meaning, to a larger or smaller degree, among other things, because different people interpret and combine the same existing elements differently – and it is precisely this fact that allows for the production of something new. This, of course, challenges certain scientific notions, such as the importance ascribed to systematic, reproducible and unbiased analysis.

If we look at the dialogical aspect of intertextuality, it refers to a number of things. First, because all academic writers are also readers, their theorizing and texts are always influenced by the texts that came before. Second, every time we read a new text it influences our interpretation of the texts that we have already read. As such, the ground continues to shift under the reader (and therefore under the writer who reads during theorizing). Third, as the historical times change, a text might be read differently and it might go in and out of fashion. Last, as readers we are aware that all texts have authors. As such, intertextuality covers a communal aspect, one we will explore in this chapter.

In Box 4.1 we present different perspectives on and concepts for understanding how reading affects us.

INTRODUCING THE FAMILY METAPHOR

In this chapter, we introduce the notion of an 'academic family' as the metaphorical expression of intertextuality. To use a metaphor means to attempt to understand one element of experience in terms of another (George Lakoff and Mark Johnson, 1980; Gareth Morgan, 1997). Theory suggests that the metaphors we, consciously or not, live and work by matter enormously (George Lakoff and Mark Johnson, 1980) because they influence the way we think, talk and act. Thus, if we think of academic theorizing as a competitive battlefield (where it is about winning or losing the publication game), then that is what we will experience and act in accordance with. If, on the other hand, we think of academic work as carried out by a family that help each other and are in it together, we will think about it differently and act differently. The family metaphor is inspired by the following statement by Andrew Van de Ven:

> I think of it as an intellectual genealogy. Point one: we cannot escape the fact that we were advised by and taught by a set of faculties at a given

school, or schools. Point two: if you keep that under a bush, that is, if you do not share that with others, people are not quite sure where you came from. If you can say I came from the University of Wisconsin and my advisor was XX, then people understand your genealogy and your location, where you came from. Then I can say, 'Oh, I hear what you are saying, but here is another point of view', which happens to be the Stanford point of view. Again, different points of view by different faculties at different locations. The last point is ... we have to be incredibly grateful that we have been schooled by people who have helped us ... So, it is like an issue of passing it on.

The quote highlights three important things. First, that the people you are taught by and the institutional norms and points of views of the places you work in shape your thinking and theorizing processes.

BOX 4.1 HOW READING AFFECTS US

It is clear from the interviews that reading is very important. At the same time, it is difficult to explain what reading does to us. The intuitive understanding is that we are affected by what we read, both by the individual text and by the sum of our reading over time. But how?

Reading is a cognitive as well as a physical activity. From the cognitive perspective, brain research shows that reading heightens brain activity and connectivity both while reading and in the subsequent resting state, improves memory and increases attention span. More bodily-oriented and phenomenological perspectives highlight that we both think and do while we read. The latter is the most unexplored: we sit in a particular place at a specific moment and the place may later be an aid to memory. Moreover, we typically say the words silently while reading, meaning that during reading the words are literally passing through us, not just as thoughts, but as sounds, rhythms and other bodily sensations. Again, this is an aid to memory, but it also causes different parts of the brain to come into play, thereby heightening the ability to think fast and to associate and bisociate.

Rita Felski (2008) suggests four ways in which reading affects us: it gives us knowledge; it facilitates recognition of ourselves and our thoughts, feelings and experiences through the words of another person; it lets us experience enchantment – for example, when we think that a book or paper is so good that we cannot initially see any flaw in it and we wish we had written it ourselves; and last, reading can shock us, when it challenges our taken-for-granted notions and reveals completely different ways of understanding a phenomenon.

Source: Inspired by Siri Hustvedt (2016) and Rita Felski (2008).

In other words, they constitute your *family background*. Second, that it is important to let other academics know what your *intellectual genealogy* is. By providing insight into the people, places and publications that have influenced your thinking, it becomes easier for them to understand your theorizing, because they understand how you are linked to the academic community and therefore what position you are speaking from. Third, in line with the family metaphor, the academic community depends on knowledge and norms being passed on from one generation to the next.

PEOPLE AND PLACES

Expressions like 'standing on the shoulders of giants' seem to suggest that all literature by well-known authors is relevant. Therefore, it is easy to overlook the role that faculty and supervisors play in future generations' theorizing through everyday interactions – where they communicate knowledge about what they do, which research topics they are interested in, and importantly, *who* they read, are inspired by and consider the giants of the field.

The interviews show clearly that much of the groundwork for the theorizing that takes place later in a researcher's career (including the choice of topics and research methods) is hugely influenced by who one works with and where one works during the formative years of the PhD and just after it. For example, Edgar Schein relates that for his PhD he wanted to go to either Harvard University or Michigan University. In the end, he chose Harvard. At the time, he did not realize how important a choice that was. If he had chosen to go to Michigan instead, he 'would have been doing surveys and totally different kind of work'. When he arrived at Harvard University, a number of research projects were taking place and he had to pick a research topic that fitted within the frame of what was already going on. This led him to focus on social influence and imitation, which much later in his career turned into an interest in organizational culture. Likewise, and as already mentioned, Barbara Czarniawska explains that for her own PhD study:

> I got two offers from two professors to join them. If I could choose I would choose social psychology ... [but] these professors got together

and the industrial psychology guy said to the social psychology guy: 'You have so many doctoral students and I don't have any, so she comes to me'. This was where I went, and I am very happy about it now, but I wasn't then.

By working with the industrial psychology professor (industrial psychology was at the time quite similar to today's business administration and management studies), Barbara Czarniawska discovered that she enjoyed doing fieldwork and the interest in this has continued to be a main focus point throughout her career.

Another thing that stands out in the interviews is the importance of the encouragement that comes from supervisors and from having face-to-face dialogues with some of the giants of one's field, during PhD seminars, department talks and conferences. David Boje says: 'I had some really good mentorship. You mentioned Karl Weick. He used to come to our university quite often and worked with my mentor, Lou Pondy ... I probably entered maybe the best PhD programme in the country at the time ... We just had people who were stars, giants.' David Boje continues the story by stating: 'but the one that really kept me on my toes was Lou Pondy', and he then talks of a handwritten letter he received and has kept. In the letter, Lou Pondy writes to David Boje that he thinks he is very good at having creative ideas and putting them into practice, and that he as his supervisor will do what he can to help him pursue that in the future.

It seems to be a common thread in the interviews that encouragement from people that one looks up to influences larger choices, such as whether to stay in academia or not, what to research and how, as well as idea development. In comparison, constructive criticism is mainly useful for the more specific work tasks of building up and refining the argument of a particular text after the idea has been hatched.

Below, we turn to publications and address the role that literature plays for theorizing. We do this by looking at literature as a work task, as dialogue, as a matter of belonging, as references, and last, by discussing literature as a challenge for new knowledge creation.

LITERATURE AS WORK TASK

For academics, it is a part of the job to know the literature of the field, in this case organizational studies, as well as the literature about the topic that one is working with, for example organizational change. It is also clear from the interviews that all contributors read a lot on a continual basis. Moreover, they read for more specific and instrumental purposes – for example, to write the theory section in a paper or to publish conceptual or review articles.

The term 'review' is often used to describe one of the important work tasks involved in theorizing. Maria J. Grant and Andrew Booth (2009, p. 92) state that to review means: 'To view, inspect, or examine a second time or again.' A review of the literature can be undertaken in several ways and numerous approaches and references on how to do a literature review exist (Sebastian Boell and Dubravka Cecez-Kecmanovic, 2010; Alessandro Liberati et al., 2009). A literature review helps the researcher identify different strands of research, major themes and research findings that already exist in the literature and to pinpoint gaps and areas for future research related to the topic of interest. Thus, from the perspective of intertextuality, a literature review is a particular genre that uses recognizable terms and elements, such as themes, findings, gaps, and so on, to interpret and combine the existing literature anew.

A literature review can be an important step toward getting an over-view of the history, authors and texts that make up a field. As such, the purpose of a literature review is to provide the foundation for producing new knowledge and for assessing whether the produced knowledge is really new or not. Moreover, a literature review helps the researcher position himself or herself in a field and to build up the argumentation of the research (Jill Jesson, Lydia Matheson and Fiona Lacey, 2011; Jane Webster and Richard Watson, 2002).

David Boje explains that in order to play the publication game, he did a systematic literature review together with some doctoral students. They took every article ever done (or that was what it felt like) on the topic they were researching, read them, used tables, did content analysis and responded to main trends. David Boje somewhat dryly remarks that it was time consuming and a lot of hard work to carry out these tasks. Andrew Van de Ven agrees that it is hard work to do a systematic literature review, but it can also be very rewarding and lead to new insights. He states:

> I have done a literature review with Scott Poole and we reviewed, Oh God, hundreds of articles on organizational change. It was tremendously satisfying to say 'You know what, after all that has been said and done it comes down to four theories: teleology, dialectics, evolution and lifecycle'. And then you get this truly satisfying, inspiring, insight!

In both examples, a systematic literature review was undertaken as a work task for the explicit purpose of publishing a paper. And full paper literature reviews that are well done are normally much appreciated by the field, because it makes other people's work easier. But what does it mean that a literature review is well done?

On the one hand, certain academic standards suggest that a literature review has to be systematic, unbiased, reproducible and relatively narrowly focused on a particular research question (Jill Jesson, Lydia Matheson and Fiona Lacey, 2011; Jane Webster and Richard Watson, 2002). On the other hand, our interview data suggests that it is the creative synthesis of the systematically selected and analysed literature that can lead to new insights – for example, through identification and naming of deep structures and drivers for organizational change as in the paper by Andrew Van de Ven and Marshall Scott Poole (2005). This way of working with the literature represents a type of creativity that seeks to write a coherent text by making already existing elements fit into a new order. As such, it is the new order – invented by the authors and often presented as four drivers, three main themes and/or 2 × 2 matrices – that is the new insight.

However, there seems to be a difference between full paper literature reviews and literature reviews that are a part of, for example, a paper about empirical research and therefore merely a section in the paper. In the first case, creative combination and theorizing are at play. In the latter case, the literature review is included because of genre convention and to frame and position the research, while it only plays a small part in the actual theorizing.

LITERATURE AS DIALOGUE

Rather than using the term 'reviewing', Kenneth Gergen suggests that it is beneficial to look at and work with the literature as dialogues that are taking place in the field:

> If you look at them more like dialogical companions, it changes your whole way of thinking ... Look at the literature as an anthropologist – this is what people are talking about. They do not have to talk about it that way. Do I want to talk about it that way? How will I do it differently? It shifts thinking.

From this perspective, namely social constructivism, the existing literature is not seen as being able to provide facts and findings about the phenomenon under study. Instead, it is analysed as dialogues that people in the field are having because they are trying to construct the phenomena they are interested in. This means that the existing literature can be read with less awe about what the giants are saying and what already exists, and more to find your own way of talking about the phenomena with the people that you wish to talk to.

Thus, a curiosity about how different people in the field talk about the phenomenon under study makes it possible to critically reflect on and choose which community of thought one would like to belong to within that field and then to show that choice to others through one's writing. This perspective shifts thinking, at least to some extent, from a focus on contributing knowledge that can be considered new from the vantage point of the existing literature to a focus on which dialogue one would like to participate in. Thus, from a dialogical perspective, participation is a relevant goal in itself, as is the wish to do one's bit to keep the dialogue fresh and interesting. As Kenneth Gergen further states: 'I would say it is kind of a personal thing. The willingness to join in becomes groundwork for significant theory. To be part of the dialogue.'

The above-mentioned quotes and points highlight that it is by taking part in a community's dialogue *as a particular person* that theorizing can happen. We explore this further in the next section.

LITERATURE AS A MATTER OF BELONGING

Above we have looked at literature as reviewing and participation. Here, we address literature as a matter of belonging. Dictionary definitions of belonging cover such things as: 'to fit in', 'be in the right place' and 'to feel right'. In addition to these, we use the term in connection with the family metaphor and as recognition in intersubjective relationships. Thus, belonging means that you (as a researcher and as a human being) recognize and feel recognized by a specific author, by a whole family of like-minded thinkers and by one or more communities.

The interviews show that it possible to conceptualize the researcher's work with literature as different kinds of engagement with text. One way of engaging with text is to have a close relationship with particular authors and texts. All contributors mention one or more authors that they have read closely and been highly influenced by. Some contributors consider these authors and their texts as dialogical partners and re-read them every now and then. For example, Tor Hernes says: 'I can always discover something new and understand something new. Every time I go to it. That happens when I go to Whitehead. And sometimes to James March as well.' Others remember a reading experience vividly and how a certain text changed their thinking. As Andrew Van de Ven states: 'In my doctoral student days it was March and Simon: *Organizations* [1958]. It was a change maker.' Likewise, Kenneth Gergen reflects: 'For me Wittgenstein would certainly be an absolute primary source … it was a major inspiration for me, and still is.' Karl Weick also refers to a *personal* canon rather than *the* canon: 'I suspect that what happens more often is that a text becomes part of one's personal canon when it becomes a continuing source of energy, ideas, connections, and literally yields "gems" no matter where it is opened.' A close relationship with a few selected authors and their texts allows both for quick inspirational reading (because the thoughts are already familiar) and in-depth thinking and theorizing infused by the ideas and concepts of a small, consciously chosen family of thinkers. Thus, the building up of a personal canon seems to be a part of becoming yourself as an academic and of finding your own voice as a writer. Or as Gaston Bachelard states (1958 [2014], p. 10): 'Every reader who re-reads a work that he likes knows that its pages *concern* him.'

Another way to engage with text is to belong to a field, and within the scope of that to get a better understanding of the topic under study. Here certain authors and texts do become a part of *the* canon. This means that you have to read them to understand how other texts use them, explicitly or through indirect allusion to them as a backdrop for thinking. For the contributors, James March's and Karl Weick's books and papers have or had status as canonical texts. Whereas the above-mentioned kind of textual engagement is driven by personal choice of what one *wants* to read, the field-oriented engagement is communal and in a sense refers to what one *has* to read or at least be aware of. This has two implications. First, all researchers have superficial knowledge about many more theoretical ideas, authors and texts than they will ever manage to read, which is an advantage from an intertextual point of view. Second, it means that much reading, and perhaps more than normally assumed, is chosen for us and driven by duty and purpose because in order to belong to a domain specific family, such as organizational studies, one has to read the texts that one finds both interesting and boring or agreeable and disagreeable. Compared to the close reading mentioned above, it can lead to a different reading strategy – which may be good or bad, depending on how you look at it. Referring to the field of sociology, Barbara Czarniawska reflects on reading strategy in this way:

> You read the beginning [of a text] and then you read the end, and only then do you decide whether you read the middle. It saves you a lot of time. But I don't know whether that is good reading. The saying goes, now everybody writes but nobody reads. It is very obvious that people read abstracts only; you can see it by the way you are quoted.

A selective reading strategy is to some extent a necessity due to the amount of extant literature on any topic. Moreover, reading for the explicit purpose of writing a specific text is necessary in order to be able to theorize about the phenomenon under study in a way that is recognizable to the field.

A third kind of textual engagement can still be exemplified by particular authors and texts, but it refers to a much broader academic family and a sense of belonging to whole thought traditions, such as the ancient Greek thinkers. As David Boje says:

> I am inspired by philosophers ... it is all Aristotle, Plato, Heidegger, Bakhtin, and lately, Karen Barad ... So I am really interested in these

philosophers and relating that to storytelling. I am very inspired by those texts. If you were here, you would see them stacked up.

From an instrumental perspective, reading literature that represents a long line of thinkers that go (way) back in time makes it possible to compare and enhance the understanding of contemporary ideas, concepts and phenomena with alternatives from the past; alternatives that may indeed be more fully articulated than current theories (Stephen Turner, 2014, p. 148). Importantly, it also has ontological implications as it makes it possible to recognize oneself as a thinker who belongs to a tradition that started long before and will continue long after one is. A reading strategy that takes the long gaze allows the theorist to draw from a deep well of ideas, make (non-obvious) connections between the past and the present, and combine existing ideas and concepts into understandings of contemporary issues.

In academia, the idiosyncratic is often frowned upon and considered a regrettable property of human cognition and behaviour. Here we suggest the opposite. Namely, that it is precisely due to close reading of a personal canon and a sense of belonging to (several) communities of thought – for example, philosophy, sociology, literary fiction – that are only vaguely or completely unrelated to the time and topics of one's field that it is possible to have ideas and develop theories that are new to the field.

Box 4.2 provides an overview of approaches to textual engagement and how they influence the theorizing process.

BOX 4.2   THREE KINDS OF TEXTUAL ENGAGEMENT

Literature in a broad sense
- Reading to become a thinker – and to belong to a tradition of thinkers
- Theorizing based on a deep well of ideas

The literature of the field
- Reading to write
- Theorizing to contribute text to the field

The personal canon
- Close reading of a few select authors
- Theorizing infused with the ideas of a small family of thinkers

---

LITERATURE AS REFERENCES

References are a part of the academic genre convention and one of those elements that highlights the intertextual nature of academic texts. The writer uses references for different reasons, and if a text is read carefully the reader can gain much information from the references that are included in a text. Inspired by the interviews, we list (some) of the ways in which references can be used:

- *Functional reasons.* References are used to avoid plagiarism and as a service to the reader so that they can locate and read the full reference.
- *Strategic and political reasons.* Certain references are included because they are or quickly become canonical texts about the topic under study, which means that they have to be cited. As Tor Hernes says: '[A]ll of a sudden they put in something and everyone else has to cite it just because it is there.' Other references might be included in anticipation of who will review the paper for publication. David Boje elaborates on this by saying that in order to play the publication game you have to 'cite all the reviewers, and the editors, and the people on the editorial boards' work and all the superstars, so you can get your article in'. His attitude to this is critical and he continues by stating that: 'by the time it gets into the press, it is not your work anymore'.
- *Positioning.* References are included to show which school of thought or strand of research your research is based on and therefore which assumptions and theoretical ideas your research is informed by. The position may be stated explicitly or the reader is expected to know that a certain reference means that the research looks at organizations from, for example, a process-oriented perspective.
- *Dialogical participation.* References are included to show which authors and texts you are in dialogue with (within a particular strand of research, again, e.g., the process perspective), in order to build on them or to challenge their views. Thus, whereas positioning shows what your research is based on, dialogical participation shows the reader who you are in the field.
- *Intellectual genealogy.* By using references to position the research and to show which dialogue you are participating in

and with what point of view, it becomes clear which texts constitute a part of your intellectual genealogy. Moreover, a part of providing insight into your intellectual genealogy is also to include references that show which family background you are coming from (e.g., supervisors, co-workers and collaborators) and which authors are a part of your personal canon and therefore significant for your theorizing.

In addition to the above-mentioned aspects, it is clear from the interviews that the researcher has to be aware which references are and are not in good currency at a given point in time in a given field. Barbara Czarniawska gives an example:

> The major problem is that very often when people move to a new field, they go to what we would call canonical stuff. This is what happened to me when I got interested in anthropology. I was reading Edmund Leach and Lévi-Strauss and all that ... there was an US anthropologist called Constance Perin. I said: 'Could you look at my book?' And she did, and said: 'But Barbara, there is a revolution going on in anthropology! This is the 1980s, we have Marcus, we have Geertz – and you are still in the 1970s!' I have noticed the same when some people come to management: they read March and Simon, 1958. It can produce interesting stuff, but they take it for what we are doing. No, this is what we were doing about 50 years ago. So, that is a problem.

Thus, an interesting dilemma arises in the sense that as a researcher you have to know the classics, because the theoretical assumptions, ideas and concepts of the canonical texts do underpin the field – and yet, you cannot necessarily cite them. As Andrew Van de Ven states: 'Now it is true that an awful lot of articles in journals never cite a paper that is older than 2000, which is really a shame for it takes you away from the classics.' This in turn can lead to a practice where a classical text is used to spice up one's thinking and writing, but without a direct reference. Thus, only the knowledgeable will be able to notice the allusion and get the extra layer of meaning from the text. Tor Hernes explains this in the following way:

> I can't publish something based on Jim's [James March's] work now. I have to stand on the shoulders of others publishing in organization journals ... I have to stand on little giants that have published something two to five years ago. Jim's work will be spicing it up. It is a bit sad, because he has written about these things before.

These reflections on how to use references and whether or not to cite the classics of a field gives rise to further considerations regarding the role of extant literature in theorizing.

LITERATURE AS A CHALLENGE

All contributors agree that reading literature – both (very) old, classic and contemporary texts – is extremely important. But it matters how you read the literature. You are in trouble:

> [...] if you look at the literature as: now we know this is the case and these are the things that are really important and this is what you must know – then you are dead. Because then all you can do is say things in that tradition that will be derivative of what is already there. You will never be very creative. You are already contained. (Kenneth Gergen)

As Kenneth Gergen points out in the quote, the existing literature can be a straitjacket that stifles your own creativity, among other things, because you start thinking that everything of relevance has already been said and that you have nothing new to add. His solution to overcome this problem is to be less concerned with whether it has already been said, if it is really new knowledge, and so on, and simply enter into the conversation and say what you want to say.

In support of this approach, Tor Hernes states: 'The thing about the field is that you are given to these reviewers. And if the reviewers don't ... reviewers only accept novelty as some kind of continuity. You have to provide that continuity to them.' In other words, even though academia is filled with talk about new knowledge production and how to make a contribution, the content and form of a given text cannot be too novel either. As mentioned, the genre convention of academic publications also makes it quite difficult to say something that is completely new, as much existing knowledge has to be repeated (but in a rewritten way, of course).

If we look at the content side, David Boje says:

> Anyway, I think that there really is very little that is new. If you go back and really read Plato, Hegel, Marx, Nietzsche, you are not going to find a lot of new after that. You can call it new if you want to; it is part of the publication game, but ...

So, the problem is that much literature and many theories and insights already exist, yet you have to contribute with new knowledge to your field using a genre convention that favours repetition. All researchers have to come to terms with this problem. Here it is relevant to remember that intertextuality stresses that a text is always based on, in dialogue with and more or less a mosaic, as Karl Weick calls it, of already existing texts. But intertextuality also highlights that literary tradition is a living organism, which thinkers and theorists can come to, eager to remember, (re)order and extend what they have read. From this perspective, writing is a way of celebrating what one has read. Moreover, it is perfectly possible that some already existing ideas, points and findings are so profound that they bear repeating – in a language that is fresh and contemporary.

In Box 4.3, Kenneth Gergen reflects critically on the giants metaphor.

BOX 4.3   IS THE GIANT METAPHOR DANGEROUS?

Kenneth Gergen states: 'I think it is a dangerous metaphor. Giants are just people who happen to be in the right place at the right time with the right metaphor. They are more like carrying a flag for people who are already committed to a certain way. I mean if you take Thomas Kuhn's *The Structure of Scientific Revolutions* [1962] that book at one time sold more copies than the Holy Bible in Western culture, but that thesis has been around for a long time. There was an earlier book ... [which] said basically the same thing, but it was premature and he didn't have a good metaphor and he wasn't at Princeton. We have made the giants. We needed something at a certain time and certain space.'

SUMMARY

All contributors agree with the message of the quote presented at the beginning of this chapter: reading is a key practice for gaining knowledge, and it is crucial when it comes to theorizing. Nevertheless, it matters what you read and how, because extant literature can be a huge source of inspiration for developing your own thinking and theoretical ideas; or it can be a straitjacket that stifles creativity and makes you think that you have nothing new to add to the already existing mass of knowledge.

In this chapter, we have focused on the metaphor of an academic family to suggest how the literature base can be approached to further your thinking rather than give rise to concerns about newness and originality. The contributors' reflections indicate that it is important to actively search for and find your own academic family – that is, the people, places and publications that make you want to think, theorize and belong.

An aspect of finding your academic family is choice. When you choose who to work with and where, your research often has to fit in, at least to some degree, with ongoing research agendas and preferred research methods. Moreover, you probably have to know the authors and texts that are considered giants at that particular institution and department. Thus, by joining a particular workplace, some choices (perhaps even many) are made for you.

Yet, other choices are driven by your personal interests and discovery of authors and texts that are highly meaningful to you. The findings in this chapter suggest that the ability to theorize is facilitated by having a foot in the literature of at least two camps: the literature of the field, which others also know well, and your own personal canon and literary preferences, which is where you – because you are you – draw your ideas from. This allows you to write about a given research topic in a way that is recognizable to the field *and* to say what you want to say; that is, to fit in *and* to be yourself as a thinker and writer. The following quote distils the central message presented in this chapter:

> Making a coherent text out of the jumble of tacit and explicit thought is the basic work of the theorist. But the choice of what to invest in and how to treat what one reads are the conditions for having theoretical ideas in the first place. And these choices are likely to have the greatest impact on one's development as a thinker. (Stephen Turner, 2014, p. 150)

BOX D DAVID MICHAEL BOJE – THE PERSONAL NARRATIVE

David was born in 1947 in Washington State, USA. He is the older brother to three siblings. At age 14, David and his family went to live for a little less than two years in Paris, where he and his younger brother learned French. After returning to the US, his parents divorced and after that he became, in this own words, 'a kind of welfare brat'.

David was the first in his family to go to college, mainly because this made it possible for him to leave the army four months earlier than scheduled. To his own as well as his teachers' surprise he graduated first in his class. After college, he was offered a scholarship and went to what is now Rider University, Princeton, followed by a master's from Illinois University. This is where he met his mentor Lou Pondy, entered the PhD programme and got 'hooked on the learning experience'. As junior faculty, David continued working together with Lou Pondy, who, inspired by anthropology and myths, encouraged David to do storytelling. The focus on storytelling became, and is, David's overall approach to both research and teaching. He brought the storytelling focus with him as assistant professor at UCLA, and later to his tenure as associate and, subsequently, full professor at Loyola Marymount University. Today he is professor of management at New Mexico State University besides being a self-proclaimed storytelling philosopher.

David's story of entering and being in academia is somehow depicted by resistance – both a personal and external resistance towards what he might, or more precisely might not, obtain. He proved them wrong. He states: 'I decided that I am just going to be critical, I am just going to be me. It doesn't do any good to pretend to be something else, playing the game, because you are not going to respect yourself afterwards.'

In a sense, David's invention of antenarrative, which is a story that is not yet in being and hence before narrative, reflects this. Just as David himself has deconstructed the idea of an academic by raising the bet and bringing into the field a personal trait of storytelling, and by that, opening up new trajectories of realization.

BOX E   ANDREW VAN DE VEN – THE PERSONAL NARRATIVE

Andrew was born in 1945 in the southern part of Netherlands. His parents had six children and his father worked as a janitor and farmer. When Andrew was five years old, the family immigrated to Canada, but after two years they found a place in Wisconsin to settle down. Despite not coming from an academic family, Andrew tells how he and his immediate siblings all became teachers – though he was the only one to move on to a PhD.

To Andrew, academia was an afterthought, based on a suggestion from Professor André Delbecq, who was his major advisor when doing his master's in business administration. As Andrew did not have other plans he began his PhD and he 'came to like it'. Subsequently, Andrew received his PhD from the University of Wisconsin at Madison in 1972. As a young scholar, together with Professor Delbecq, he developed the world-leading brainstorming technique, the nominal group technique, a method that emerged as an anomaly when looking at something else, that is, doing neighbourhood studies. The aspect of finding something different from what one is searching for seems very aligned with Andrew's curiosity towards the phenomenon in front of him and his openness towards what the phenomenon might reveal. So, if you are not able to fully plan what to look for, the implication is that you need to look long enough to get in-depth insights. This temporal aspect has been apparent throughout Andrew's career as he has primarily been doing longitudinal studies – be that on organizational assessment or innovation management.

Andrew's focus on practice has also led him towards reflections on the practice of academia itself. His concern with ongoing learning, and herein teaching, both in regard to himself and others, is manifested in his book from 2007 called *Engaged Scholarship: A Guide for Organizational and Social Research*. Being an engaged scholar is in Andrew's view to obtain a holistic understanding of what you are studying, to be open in your theoretical and methodological approach, and to continuously communicate with your audience.

Looking back, Andrew expresses gratitude for his opportunity to have had an academic career – which he perceives the most exciting career he could have ever imagined. With a laugh, he states: 'For me, being an academic feels like I have been retired all my life.'

5. Making a contribution

[B]eing human always points, and is directed, to something or someone
other than oneself – be it a meaning to fulfil or another human being
to encounter.
(Viktor E. Frankl, 1963, p. 115)

In the previous chapter, we looked at academic genealogy through
the lens of the family metaphor. In this chapter, we elaborate even
further on this perspective by exploring perceptions of what a
theoretical contribution is and how contributing is deeply interlinked
with temporal aspects.

When we talk about a theoretical contribution, it often refers to the
publication of a piece of writing that adds new understandings and
ideas to the existing literature base. From the previous chapters in
this book, it is clear that it takes time to write a coherent text that
actually constitutes a theoretical contribution. Moreover, the interviewees consider contribution in a broad sense, from publications,
through societal impact, to influencing an individual. But it seems
that what really matters to the interviewees are the latter two. Thus, it
is not until the theoretical ideas make a difference for other people –
including other researchers as well as practitioners – that they really
count as a contribution.

The concepts of rigour and relevance are often used to define what
it means to make a contribution, emphasizing that there may be a
gap between academia and practice and that it can be necessary to
distinguish between good research and useful knowledge (Gerard
Hodgkinson and Denise Rousseau, 2009; Alfred Kieser and Lars
Leiner, 2009). But, in this chapter, we wish to explore the topic
in another way by drawing on the concept of time. We use time
to understand the role that temporal aspects, such as clock time,
ripe moments and academic maturity, play in making a theoretical
contribution. The focus on time allows for a dynamic perspective that

includes other people as co-creators, thereby making theory 'an open space' (Kenneth Gergen). This denotes that a published theory is a theory-in-the-making that someone else can pick up, have something to say about and/or put to practical use one way or the other. As such, theorizing and contributing are not just things that the author does nor are they things that have endpoints. Instead, they can be seen as collaborative activities that unfold in time.

SETTING THE SCENE

In this chapter, we highlight that it takes *a long time* to make a theoretical contribution. Thus, a key point in this chapter is to acknowledge that time matters for theorizing.

First, we can think of time as a condition, that is, we are always right here right now in the present. Second, time can be seen as a dimension of being, that is, we can experience time differently – as passing slowly or flying by, as a scarce resource, and so on. Moreover, there are two recognized conceptualizations of time: time as objective, existing outside the human mind, and time as subjective and mind-dependent (Annawat Bunnag, 2017). But the difference between objective and subjective perceptions of time is not clear-cut. After Albert Einstein introduced the theory of relativity, even the perception of time as absolute was shattered. If the speed of light is the overarching absolute, both time and space must be relative to this. From a natural science perspective, the implication is that the past, present and future are perceived to be simultaneous dimensions of the same phenomenon – time. Time is not flowing, time is just there. With this understanding, time 'collapses' and the past and the future are seen as embedded in the present.

To us as social scientists (or at least to us as authors) this is a bit abstract. However, translated to our purposes, this can, for example, be understood in the following way: the past is here right now in the form of existing literature and ideas that the theorist can draw on while sitting down to write a text in the present, a text that anticipates the future – that is, who will read it and what will be relevant for them in their (work) lives in the future. Moreover, by making a distinction between chronological and kairotic time the 'time collapse' becomes more applicable. The distinction stems from ancient Greek, where chronological time refers to (quantitative) *clock time*, that is, time as something that can be measured, while kairotic time refers to (qualitative) moments in time, that is, defining or *right moments* (Barbara Czarniawska, 2004). In this chapter, we use the distinction between chronological and kairotic to understand the interviewees' statements and stories of how contributions are realized over time, within specific time periods, and in certain moments in time.

TEMPORAL ASPECTS IN RESEARCH AND REALIZATION PROCESSES

In Chapter 3, we showed, and argued, that research is always contemporary – that is, embedded in and marked by the historical times in which it is conducted. However, time is also a key aspect of the research process and activities as such, as well as of the realization processes, which eventually lead to theoretical contributions. Of course, time is an integral part of all process-oriented researchers' theories, because processes unfold in time, but the notions of time that they draw on seem to differ.

Some contributors, especially Barbara Czarniawska and David Boje, have worked with narratives and storytelling respectively, seeing narratives as constitutive for organizing. Narratives can be applied both as a research methodology and as a way of theorizing about organizations. When applying a narrative mindset, time is a prominent feature with regard to understanding the narratives themselves, which are seen as sequential accounts with a start, a middle and an ending that evolve around events that create a plot. Moreover, time is central with regard to seeing stories as social glue, knitting together shared and individual perceptions of past, present and future in organizations. In this manner, narrative research can embrace both chronological and kairotic time perspectives towards understanding the phenomenon under study. Time can also be an explicit part of the proposed theoretical concepts. For example, time plays an important role in Karl Weick's theory about sensemaking in organizations – which is retrospective in nature. In his interview, he distinguishes between short-term sensemaking and long-term meaning making:

The process of sensemaking is focused on short-term, satisfactory (plausible), provisional understandings that enable a person or group to keep going and to engage in further actions that refine and update initial hunches. As one updates provisional understandings, this revising may engage deeper, more long-term experiences, in which case sensemaking blends into meaning making. This movement from sense to meaning is also reversible. Meanings collapse and sensemaking itself can become problematic.

In general, notions such as short-term, long-term, retrospective, reversibility and circularity seem to be key to Karl Weick's theory development.

Likewise, Tor Hernes is interested in time and especially in the concept of organizational becoming. He explains:

I have been working on time and temporality. And this is what I found – after several years of working or thinking about these things, now what we need to think about is time, becoming in time. But it took years for me to arrive at that. And this is where I will be working for the next ten years, because there is so much to do. It resonates with so much, and we can do so much, we can speak to the strategy people, we can speak to historians. We now want to set up a centre for organizational time here.

Thus, Tor Hernes applies time as an explicit theoretical perspective for understanding the research topic – organizations – while at the same time pinpointing that his own realization processes also take time.

To Andrew Van de Ven, time is a means to reveal processual aspects of innovation and change. In his case, longitudinal studies ensure a dual process where the methodological choice and his own process of insights are highly intertwined. In this manner, longitudinal studies support both certain types of realizations about the phenomenon and a personal development towards becoming an expert on the subject. Edgar Schein also links time and thorough research by stressing how good and extensive studies need time and freedom to evolve. Likewise, Geert Hofstede emphasizes that realizations happen over time – as mentioned earlier, the notion of cultural dimensions emerged because he kept looking at the same phenomena: differing perceptions in different cultural contexts. Geert Hofstede further mentions how he searched for an audience with whom to discuss his findings and went in a direction where he could work with experienced managers. He had expected to do so for two years; however, to his own surprise, he ended up spending six years on this because the subject matter led him in new directions. The point in Geert Hofstede's case is that despite being in diverse workplaces he remained preoccupied with a certain question – which only time could fully unfold.

TEN-YEAR TIME LOOPS

Following the above examples, several interviewees stress that it can easily take ten years or more to make a theoretical contribution. First, you have to get the idea and do the research, including empirical work, in-depth reading and abductive reasoning. This takes time. Then you have to write a coherent text, which is an essential part of theorizing as it is often during writing that the argument becomes solid and the details are thought through. Therefore, writing in itself can take several months if it is a paper, or years if it is a book. Thereafter, the text has to be reviewed, typically several times, and even then publication is just the first step towards making a contribution. David Boje explains:

> I don't know if you know, but it takes ten years to get a new theory into these places [journals]. First you have to come up with the concept and then someone has to pick it up and publish about it in top journals and now people are publishing about it [antenarrative] in good tier-journals. And some people contact me with pieces about storytelling and we slip the word antenarrative in there, but not too much to piss off the reviewers. And we are now also working on a more caring perspective, using philosophers and pragmatism ... and now it is a pretty robust theory. But it has taken a lot of time.

David Boje's conceptualization of what it means, and especially what it takes to make a contribution differs quite a lot from the notion that the author writes a text, which then constitutes a contribution. Instead a more open-ended, collaborative and distributed process is suggested; one where the author proposes one or more theoretical ideas that others can become interested in, wish to extend (or argue against) and publish about – and only after several people have devoted their time, skills and thinking to develop the ideas further can it be considered a robust theory.

This has a number of implications. First, it suggests that it is relevant for the theorist to take into account what others are interested in and care about. Or as Kenneth Gergen says: 'There are a lot of ways to theorize. I ask myself: "What moves people?"' Moreover, it goes against expectations and language use where it is more or less explicitly assumed that a PhD thesis makes a contribution in itself or that an assistant professor can make a theoretical contribution to the field within a limited number of years. It also questions the focus on citations as a relevant criterion for hiring associate professors, because, as Tor Hernes points out in the quote below, more often than not it takes years before people have had time to incorporate your ideas into their own work:

> It takes ten years. I like to think in 10–15-year cycles. From when you start something it takes you years, it takes years to get a paper published, it takes years for someone to cite it. It takes years to get a book out, to get an edited volume, to get conference tracks. Before things begin to take off it is easily ten years.

The above quotes show that in addition to the work that goes before publication, there is also work to be done after publication in order for a theory to take off. This includes going to conferences to make people aware of your ideas, hosting conference tracks (including writing calls-for-papers, receiving and ensuring that papers about the topic are reviewed and accepted), co-authoring papers or editing books or special issues about the topics. In other words, if you are really interested in your ideas, you have to bring them out into the world and make it both possible and desirable for people to connect with them through activities such as reading, writing, talking, teaching and collaborating.

Thus, all interviewees are aware that it takes a lot of time and research effort to get to the stage where your ideas are circulating in the world. But, whether a theory strikes a chord with academic and/or practitioner communities also depends on what is happening during a specific time period and what occupies the collective consciousness and is considered interesting and contemporary.

FASHION AND FADS

Most interviewees are driven by an urge to understand phenomena
as they are currently exposed. Thus, they try to stay attuned to what
is in and out of fashion at a given point in time – but still with an
unambiguous awareness of the phenomenon's position in a historical and cultural context. Moreover, they are cognizant that what is
topical at a given period in time frames academic research and hence
determines whether the research can be published and generate interest or not. In line with this, Barbara Czarniawska refers to fashion as
a major societal mechanism:

> No matter how much people criticize it [fashion] and call it irrational or
> whatever, it was there, it is here, and it is going to be there, it will continue.
> Why? That is because what organization change agents are saying, that
> people are against change, is nonsense. If people were against change
> we would be sitting in caves. People love change, but not change that is
> imposed on them against their will. So fashion is never really new – if
> it were, it would have to come from another planet. It must be a clever
> combination of what is recognizable and what is new, because otherwise
> it is frightening or boring.

As the excerpt reveals, a new theoretical idea or concept must refer
back to something to make sense at a specific time period. Thus,
the point is that thoughts and ideas go around in circles and can
be recycled, yet they are never exactly the same because the times
have changed since they were last in fashion. With a glint in her eye,
Barbara Czarniawska suggests:

> Fashion sort of recovers things. There are people who are forgotten and
> all of a sudden they are remembered. You know Mary Parker Follett, I
> knew nothing of her until the late 1980s when she was again fashionable.
> People say this is the way of making a career: find, or locate, a forgot-
> ten anthropologist, sociologist, somebody you discovered. Think about
> Mary Douglas who rediscovered Ludwik Fleck. Think about Bruno
> Latour, who rediscovered Gabriel Tarde – it is not so bad!

An implication of this is that academic fashion and fads are a condition and consequently nothing to fight against. Barbara Czarniawska
therefore also suggests that junior researchers best not specialize to
a degree where they will not be prepared when fashion changes. In a
similar vein, Kenneth Gergen relates how his own publication, *The
Saturated Self* (1991), hit at a time where people were concerned

with the issues exposed in the book, whereas as a reviewer he has also seen high-quality thoughts on a subject not getting published, solely 'because nobody cared anymore'. Fashion can also more directly frame the topic under study. As Edgar Schein recalls, 'When I arrived at MIT in 1956, corporate brainwashing was *the* topic!' Since Edgar Schein as a social psychologist had studied brainwashing, MIT wanted to bring him in and focus on business. He therefore states that his research agenda was handed to him based on what was popular in those days.

To sum up, a thought and a theoretical idea are influenced by the past, anchored in historical time and shaped by an anticipated future, while also being conditioned by what is academically fashionable. Thus, theorizing happens *in* time. Moreover, expertise in theorizing matures *over* time through individual processes of perfecting one's skills and work practices as a thinker and theorist.

ACADEMIC MATURITY

Malcolm Gladwell (2008) suggests that it takes 10 000 hours, or roughly ten years, of practice to become really good at something. Likewise, Stuart and Hubert Dreyfus's theory (1980) delineates the progression in skills (including assimilation of existing knowledge and an ability to read situations and find suitable solutions) that one goes through as one moves from being a novice to an expert. Both theories draw attention to the fact that it takes time, practice and skill development to become an expert at something. And as the previous chapters in this book have shown, as a researcher there are many things you have to become good at before you are able to theorize about a subject. These include:

- finding, reading and creating an overview of relevant literature;
- getting to know one or more theories in depth;
- doing empirical studies, that is, knowing, choosing among, and applying empirical data collection and analysis methods;
- thinking about the research topic with the help of existing literature, theory, empirical data, your own life experiences and other material that you have at hand or that are present in your life world – and based on these ingredients, developing your own ideas about the phenomenon under study;

- writing a coherent text that conveys your thoughts and line of argument in a way that resonates with the reader.

Some of the above-mentioned skills are general, developed as a part of one's academic craftsmanship over time and therefore reusable across research topics and projects. In addition to these general skills, one has to think deep, long and hard about the particular subject that one is researching and aiming to theorize about. Or as Karl Weick (2014) states, theorizing is about racking one's brain in order to say something profound, surprising and interesting about the subject.

Tor Hernes gives an example that illustrates the long-term time perspective that deep thinking and theory development might require: 'I was in the committee this year. And we gave it to Lauren, she works in sociology and law, she is from Berkeley University. And she told me, before we went up to the stage, that it actually took her 20 years. Not writing, but the very ideas that are in this book took her 20 years.'

Based on the above, there are two things that are worth pointing out. One thing is that while many aspects of academic craftsmanship can be taught through books, papers and courses, the core of theorizing – namely the actual thinking and idea development – is idiosyncratic and therefore difficult to articulate as practices that can be passed on to others. The only practice that seems to capture this aspect of theorizing is – give it time. The second point is that because it takes a long time to develop your thinking about a particular research topic, several interviewees plan to work in ten-year cycles. They tend to spend ten years of research to become really good at one topic before they move on to the next, somewhat related research theme. For example, Andrew Van de Ven explains:

> The phenomena I have been studying over time are change, organizational change and innovation and those kinds of issues ... you know, it takes about ten years to become world-class at any subject. Ten years of dedicated, persistent hard work. Where you have many trials and errors. I have seen myself as being lucky enough to become world class at about four or five subjects [over the course of my career]. Every subject is seen as ... they are published in a series of texts and articles, as a set of books that you author and put together ... you are not just stopping after your first publication, which will not be world class.

It seems reasonable to distinguish between academic craftsmanship, which relates to methods and practices, becoming an expert at a particular subject and becoming a good theorist. The latter seems to be a cumulative skill that develops as one becomes good at the academic craft and has worked in-depth with one or a few selected research topics. To support this claim, we can see that the interviewees did not publish their major renowned work until later in their career.

All contributors were in their late forties or fifties when they wrote the book they are most known for. To exemplify, Geert Hofstede was 55 years old when *Culture's Consequences: International Differences in Work-related Values* was published in 1983, Tor Hernes was 53 years old when *A Process Theory of Organization* was published in 2014, Karl Weick was 59 years old when *Sensemaking in Organizations* was published in 1995 and finally, Edgar Schein was 57 years old when *Organizational Culture and Leadership* met the market in 1985.

In Box 5.1, Kenneth Gergen describes characteristics of the early, middle and late academic career stages as he has experienced them. Moreover, he explains that what he has considered a contribution has changed over time as he has matured as an academic.

BOX 5.1   THE THRILL OF HAVING AN ACADEMIC CAREER

Kenneth Gergen states: 'What is thrilling depends on where you are in your career. Initially, what was thrilling was simply making it in the career; that is, having articles published and having a job. I got this prized job at Harvard as my first position and I had articles published and it was like "Wow". It was all about just finding a niche for yourself. There is a second thing that kicks in after that, which I'm not proud of, but it is there and it is the thrill of competition with other people in your field. Everybody is trying to have their work cited, to have money, to have the most graduate students. It is a contest ... that is the way we were brought up and there was a certain thrill in that. Now that changes, because after a while that seems sort of trivial. And that's when sort of mid-career, later in my career I think, "What is this contributing to the world?", "Who cares?" And then what really has been important to me in the last 30 years is making a difference outside the academic community and contributing something to world change, world betterment. That has been really thrilling and I think a much more mature sense of thrill.'

CONTRIBUTING TO ONESELF AND TO OTHERS

At its starting point research is (also) a selfish pursuit. The researcher wants to read, write, think – wants to know. In his book *Man's Search for Meaning*, Victor E. Frankl states: 'What man actually needs is not a tensionless state but rather the striving and struggling for a worthwhile goal, a freely chosen task' (Frankl, 1963, p. 110). A freely chosen task gives a certain type of passion; a passion that may be necessary for the long haul that theorizing entails. Edgar Schein describes such a freely chosen task:

> I decided to write about process consultation with a set of stories and when it comes to culture, I decided to write it in a way that makes sense to me. Primarily it has to make sense to me. Then the market tells me that it also makes sense to other people. People said: 'When I read *Process Consultation* [1969, 1999], I finally understood what I do ... '. My story enabled other people to see themselves in the story.

The quote shows the close link between the slow organic growth of understanding that happens in chronological time as the researcher writes about the subject and the defining moments in kairotic time where the writer becomes aware that he or she has contributed to somebody. There are several examples in the interview material where it becomes clear that to a large extent it is these defining moments that give meaning to and justify the researcher's work as well as the time and effort that the work took. Andrew Van de Ven remembers the following episode:

> For example, in the neighbourhood block meetings, after the fourth group meeting as we began to develop the nominal group technique, I can remember, now this is about 45 years ago, an old gentleman coming up to me saying, 'You know, this is the first time in my life where I have felt that I could speak my mind'. Now what more can you ask of a life? ... For me it is not the number of citations, or the number of publications, or where or what journal that publishes me, it is to hear that gentleman telling me that I have changed his life.

When asked about which contribution he is proud of, Geert Hofstede relates similar stories of encountering specific people that tell him that he has helped them understand aspects of their lives that they would otherwise not have understood. Answering the same question, David Boje says: 'I have really enjoyed working with students and faculty. I like that a lot. In terms of writing, the antenarrative book of 2001 was fun.' Again, the combination of writing to contribute to oneself as well as to other people, in David Boje's example to other researchers, stands out as what defines what it means to make a contribution.

In Box 5.2, Geert Hofstede reflects on what it means to make a contribution at an individual level.

BOX 5.2 MAKING A *REAL* CONTRIBUTION

Geert Hofstede states: 'My interest has been in the practical use of my work. Many colleagues at the university couldn't care less about it. They didn't really think that what they were doing should have a practical use. I still come across people who only use my work for number crunching. Fortunately, I also meet people who sit down, read my books and tell me it has changed their lives.

One of my nicest stories is that when I worked in Hong Kong we met a Chinese husband with a Japanese wife. The moment the Chinese husband had left the room the Japanese wife said: "You know, you have saved our marriage." And I said it sounded nice and asked: "How did I do that?" And she said: "Well, I noticed that if my husband goes out in the evening for some meeting and he is late, he never telephones to tell me that he will be late. So, I thought that he was not interested in me anymore. And then I started reading your books, and I found that there is a big difference between Japanese and Chinese culture. The Japanese have a strong uncertainty avoidance and the Chinese have a weak uncertainty avoidance. So, he still loves me, but our difference is cultural." That is one story that shows me – what you have been doing at least has some use for some people!'

Different researchers have different opinions about what theory is and what a theory looks like. However, the interviewees we have talked to seem to agree that theories that have a societal impact and that contribute to world betterment often start by making it possible for specific people in specific relationships to have better conversations with each other, and to voice their opinion in the different contextual situations in which they find themselves. As Kenneth Gergen says:

[I]f I have a theory that is so abstract that you cannot put it into a conversation, it is probably not doing anything ... For me, you have to theorize in a way that comes out and can be taken up in a conversation. I am not interested in a lot of enormous, complex propositions that are interrelated and where I have made sure that I am guarded against everybody who ever said anything, so it is perfect – because no one will use it. For me it is: 'Say something that is strong and that people can use in some way'.

SUMMARY

In this chapter, we looked into how temporal aspects such as clock time, ripe moments and academic maturity influence theorizing in general and making a theoretical contribution specifically.

When considering chronological time, the interview material revealed a shared experience and understanding of a certain academic circularity, which exposes itself as a sort of magical 'ten-year rule'. Two aspects are at stake: a collective and an individual one. The collective aspect has to do with the process of publishing your theoretical ideas and making them live in the world. All the interlinked processes such as reviewing, editing, disseminating by presentations, getting and giving feedback and striking a chord that is popular are estimated to take ten years. The individual aspect involves developing and refining your competences as a researcher and thinker. Here the same time period prevails – that you have to stick to the same topic for ten years to become really good at it. In addition to chronological time we see kairotic time aspects as part of theorizing. These are the defining moments of the process, be they a realization or a concrete experience of having contributed to a specific person or setting.

Based on insights from the interviews we suggest a broad definition of what it means to make a theoretical contribution – a definition that goes well beyond the published text and looks at the various ways in which theoretical ideas are at work *in* and *over* time and how they contribute to either theory-in-the-making, to practice or to individuals. And as such also become a contribution to yourself as researcher.

Barbara Czarniawska reflects:

> But no one can predict it, which metaphor [or theory] will catch on and which will not. It is like with all fashions. Everybody is trying, but nobody really knows what is going to happen. And then everybody is very wise afterwards, sort of rationalizing, saying yes, of course, but they don't know it beforehand.

Barbara Czarniawska's statement emphasizes the earlier mentioned point that choice and chance are intertwined aspects of an academic (or perhaps any) career. This might be important to acknowledge, especially for young scholars, in order to balance between deliberate and strategic choices and the urge to go with a hunch. Especially since the hunch might become the contribution that in retrospect will matter the most for you as both theorist and person.

BOX F   KENNETH GERGEN – THE PERSONAL NARRATIVE

Kenneth was born in 1934 in the United States into academia. His father was a university professor in mathematics and Kenneth therefore grew up in a community of professors and professors' children. Out of four sons, both his younger brother, David Gergen, and himself became professors. But to Kenneth this was not of particular interest in his early years – until accepted into graduate school he thought about doing theatre.

Nevertheless, Kenneth reasons that he stayed in academia because university professors encouraged him, because he enjoys thinking and finally because he saw what the alternatives were. He was never really inclined to follow his friends into business practice. Thus, after two years of military service, he went directly to graduate school and in his own words 'never looked back'. Kenneth received his PhD in psychology in 1963 from Duke University, and started directly as an assistant professor at Harvard University. In 1967, Kenneth took a position at Swarthmore College, Pennsylvania, and in addition to various positions as visiting professor across Europe and the United States, he is now professor emeritus of psychology and senior research professor at Swarthmore.

Kenneth Gergen has been profoundly concerned with social interaction and how knowledge is socially constructed. The implication is an urge to understand alternatives to what is taken for granted and, as such, his research has been meta-theoretical in the sense that it transcends specific research fields. Later he has focused on how constructionist ideas can be put into dialogue with practice so the interplay between academia and practice can be beneficial to both domains, but also to society at large.

This wish for mutual enrichment between scholars and professionals resulted in the non-profit organization The Taos Institute, founded by Kenneth and his wife Mary (now professor emeritus at Penn State University) in 1993. The theoretical base is social constructionism and Kenneth's most recent focus is positive ageing. Together with Mary he seeks to change the picture of ageing from decline to seeing the whole life span as continuous development. To reinvent ageing Kenneth again invites dialogue: 'How do you create a reality of pros and something to look forward to? So, you feel really lucky that you get there?'

BOX G   EDGAR SCHEIN – THE PERSONAL NARRATIVE

Edgar was born in 1928 in Switzerland. Before moving to America at the age of ten he had lived six years in Switzerland, three years in the Soviet Union and one year in Prague, in today's Czech Republic.

Edgar's father was a professor of physics and despite some difficulty figuring out what to study Edgar never thought of anything else than becoming a professor himself. On a biology course, he 'ran into psychology', got interested and decided to study it. Edgar connects his choice of profession with the following two aspects: being raised as an only child and living in different countries in his early childhood. When raised in different places, to listen and to observe become necessities. Edgar states that it made him become aware since he also had to keep a distance – learning to be adaptable whilst not really being embedded in the different cultures of his childhood homes. Additionally, being an only child, Edgar needed to constantly build relationships, a matter that made him concerned with what goes on between people, as both a competence and a curiosity. Therefore, Edgar refers to his obsession with hearing, seeing and analysing as a coping strategy of his youth, but also he comprehends the ability to see things from different perspectives as an advantage when having an academic career.

Edgar decided to do a PhD at Harvard University after they started to combine sociology, anthropology and psychology, which he found very intriguing. Consequently, he received his PhD in social psychology from Harvard University in 1952. Since he was anxious to get drafted, Edgar joined a programme where he immediately became an officer if he agreed to be an army psychologist for three to four years – so being under army auspices he continued to work with his interest in social influence, and later imitation. As a young postdoctoral student Edgar obtained a position at the Walter Reed Army Institute of Research, and he relates how he became concerned with the topic of institutions since he was fortunate to work with Leon Festinger and Erving Goffman, who were both doing consultancy there. Leaving the army, Edgar arrived at MIT in 1956, and made his entrance into business and management, which he recalls was a totally blank slate in his mind at that time.

Across research foci, Edgar's main interest has always been people and the human side of organizing. This is mirrored in his work on organizational culture that seems to encompass his curiosity towards experiments, relationships and being a (helpful) process facilitator.

6.   Key points and practices

[R]ecognition is an indispensable moment in interpretation.
(Rita Felski, 2008, p. 133)

We started out by proposing the metaphors of a mirror room and echo chamber as the foundation for investigating processes and practices of theorizing of whom we, our students and our colleagues believe to be the giants within organizational research. Our wish has been to present the thoughts and reflections of the contributors to the reader to prepare the ground for considerations about his or her own ways of, and voice in, theorizing. Through the extensive use of quotes, the contributors' personal stories of being in academia and sound bites on relevant concepts and themes from the interview data, we hope the point has become clear that theorizing is not a step-wise approach to be adopted, but a creative individual and collective process to engage in.

In this chapter, we will sum up the key points with regard to perceptions of theory and conditions for theorizing. Moreover, we reflect upon the inherent critique of the current academic system in the interview material and finally make some concluding remarks.

REFLECTIONS ON THEORIZING

As shown in Chapter 2, the contributors have different ways of referring to theory, ranging from analytical concepts, mental models, logical claims, plots, and ontological alternatives. Despite differences in terminology, the shared perception is that we apply and develop theories, in the mentioned understandings, to reduce complexity and to better understand the phenomena we are looking at. As such, the cogency of a theory is related to either its profoundness, the way it cuts to the bone and says something solid and thorough, or its power to create an overview that makes it easier to see the big picture. Following this, the contributors do not seem to be especially concerned with categorizing theory as either grand theories or middle-range theories.

So, what is it that calls for thinking (Martin Heidegger, 1968 [2004])? A shared characteristic of all contributors is that they are preoccupied with the world and therein questions regarding being, organizing and relations. But their preoccupations take different forms – as a focus on academic craftsmanship (in Andrew Van de Ven's terms, engaged scholarship); as an urge to look in depth into a specific topic (such as Geert Hofstede's ongoing focus on cultural matters); by sticking to a particular approach (like David Boje who lets storytelling permeate his private and professional life); or as an inclination to create new fields or open up existing ones. The latter aspects reflect both Tor Hernes's interest in bringing new concepts into the field of organizing and Kenneth Gergen's focus on social constructivism as an overall game changer in prevalent perceptions inside and outside academia. Hence, the underlying basis for what to look at, and theorize about, is partly triggered by a personal passion, wonder or interest.

Another key aspect of theory and theorizing is time. We see three main issues here:

- First, your personal time perspective seems to influence the understanding of and approach to knowledge production. A long-term time perspective makes knowledge production an open-ended process that includes various actors, that is, 'me and many others', while a short-term perspective seems to increase result orientation and text publication of most often one actor, that is, 'me and my work'. The contributors are all process oriented, taking a long-term time perspective on knowledge creation, while the short-term perspective is primarily related to writing practices and individual dissemination of knowledge (in contrast to co-creation of knowledge).
- Second, time is about maturity as a thinker. We can tell that developing a voice that is loud enough to reach a wide audience depends on the time you spend with the subject under scrutiny and the feedback that you receive while doing so. The

stories of the contributors show that it takes more or less a decade to both understand something thoroughly and to make an argument come alive.

● Last, time is a condition when playing the academic game. The lifespan of a theory is highly dependent on an audience, even though it need not be a contemporary one. In Chapter 5, the feature of circularity came to the fore by the contributors' emphasis on academic fads and fashion. Thus, a certain theory can come back into fashion or a theory can be in line with what is current both within and outside academia – matters you cannot fully master or be in control of, since they are also contingent on a share of luck.

CONDITIONS FOR THEORIZING

Theorizing is dialogical in nature since theory is always negotiated and contested with somebody – be that in person or in literature. In continuation thereof, the interviews revealed that a facet of engaging in theorizing is anxiety. The contributors distinguish between the following different forms: a fear of not getting there with regard to making a consistent, beautiful argument; an existential doubt in yourself; an external fear of not being accepted in the academic domain one addresses; and anxiety as a driver for showing the world and yourself that you are capable. As such, anxiety, or *angst*, is an undercurrent that is both a precondition for thinking that is meant to be exposed to others, and something to be balanced, so it does not overwhelm you.

To not become too anxious due to distraction, lack of time and inspiration, or all of the above, the contributors have developed practices that support their creativity and thinking processes. We have identified the following: making appointments with yourself; structuring your workday; physical movement; reading in the language you are going to write in; reading own text pieces or well-written pieces of others; and more generally reading broadly. Basically, it comes down to the following two main points: acknowledging that just being placed in front of the computer looking at the cursor does not in itself lead to creativity and that you need to, in Barbara Czarniawska's words, diagnose yourself and come to know your own strengths, weaknesses and habits and make conditions for inspiration and thinking accordingly.

Another central condition for theorizing is belonging. The contributors' reflections indicate that it is important to actively search for and find your own academic family – the people, places and publications that make you think and that make you feel you belong to one or more communities, or that you wish to belong to them. Finding such a family is both conditioned by exogenous and endogenous circumstances: exogenous such as the place you study, your workplace, the supervisors you are assigned and outer influence of friends, family and country of birth and/or residence; endogenous as the inner motivation to become the thinker you would like to be and the more deliberate actions you take to get there, the literature you read, the discussions you engage in, the positions you apply for. Of course, these two types of circumstances cannot be separated, but the interviews illustrate that finding your academic family is marked by both chance and choice.

As might be evident at this moment, it has become a point in itself that behind theories and analytical concepts there are people. By inquiring into the work lives of the contributors, we ended up with a number of interviews that were more personal than expected. However, on reflection it is not surprising that the experience of being in academia, the research topics that emerge, the use of practices that facilitate theorizing and the people you meet and are inspired by are intertwined features linked to personal traits, subjective contexts, interests and desires.

To exemplify, one of these unexpected conditions for theorizing that became apparent when talking to Andrew Van de Ven and Geert Hofstede was love. It was a very fine experience for us to hear how they both in one of their first comments on their work emphasized the role of their families. To both of them a well-functioning family and a long-lasting marriage have laid the ground for their own creativity and as such the understanding of academic career or work life is in retrospect deeply interwoven with their personal life conditions. Another pattern that emerged from the interviews was that most contributors have lived, studied or travelled in several countries, a characteristic that seems to influence their ability to stay open towards new phenomena and to let changes in perspective trigger what to look at and for. Even though we cannot all move around the world the capacity of staying curious and open towards displacements can be something to strive for.

CRITICAL REFLECTIONS

Despite our focus on inspiration and an urge to highlight the thrill of engaging in thinking processes, we cannot oversee a critique of the academic system that is both explicitly and implicitly present in the interview data. Some contributors are aware that they refer back to a time with different work conditions than those of today, whereas others explicitly stress the change that they have experienced while still being in academia. The interviews have made it clear that theorizing, and the contribution of this process, is highly dependent on the ability to structure associations and bisociations – in Barbara Czarniawska's terms. We translate this into reading broadly, engaging in constructive dialogue with people inside and outside your domain, spending time crossing fields (both in mind and body), making time to play with thoughts and ideas and then structuring these inputs so they become not just available, but more importantly, also interesting and inspiring to others. However, this leads to the essential question – does the current academic review and reward system support such activities?

We see two main issues at stake: the expectation of identifying a research gap and a narrow focus on what a contribution is. In our experience, these two aspects are especially central and perhaps most problematic when you are a junior researcher trying to find your own way alongside developing your skills as researcher and thinker.

If we look at the insights from the interviews, the idea of identifying a gap in the literature is an illusion. A research gap sounds like there is an empty space waiting to be filled, whereas in (inspired) research we draw on each other's work, we discuss it, we think further and we rethink it. Therefore, it might be fruitful to instead think and talk in terms of identifying research questions that are explicitly relevant to somebody (be it researchers and/or practitioners) and that not only add to but also expand the existing knowledge base. Another trap of the gap metaphor is the obvious question of whether the gap needs to be filled at all – or as a senior researcher dryly commented on one of our PhD courses: 'a research gap might just exist because the topic is not interesting enough to explore'.

Furthermore, the current review system seems somehow to be based on the underlying assumption that identifying a gap necessarily leads to a contribution – in the sense that the contribution is the filler. We have for years met the following two questions from senior researchers: 'What is your contribution?' 'Which knowledge base do you contribute to?' These common questions, at least in our own experience, are based on the conviction that early on in your writing and thinking process you have identified the aforementioned gap and now know exactly what your answer will be and to whom. In this manner, the current academic system favours answers over good, relevant, surprising, deep questions. Furthermore, when giving the answer precedence there is little room and time to refine, change or even dismiss the question you set out to explore.

This narrow understanding of what a contribution is and how it is delivered stands in contrast to the contributors' experience of their main contribution. It can be a journal article or a more in-depth piece of work presented in a book, but in addition to the written contributions, the contributions to practice and/or to individuals seem to matter the most.

Early in our career as researchers, we are currently trained in a specific form of academic craftsmanship that approves written production in form of journal articles – which then implies that the editorial board of the journal sets the frame for the writing and dissemination style. We find this training pretty instrumental and outcome-oriented in contrast to the creative skills and the process orientation we find among the contributors, especially since their practices underscore that the process of realization is not linear – you might write on a hunch and through that write the realization into existence. Moreover, the range of the argument is not fully developed in your first paper on the topic, but needs refinement in the form of feedback, personal thinking and simply just by getting a life outside your own head. A process that takes time – and that requires *both* academic craftsmanship *and* idiosyncratic creativity.

In Box 6.1, David Boje critically reflects on the current situation in academia.

BOX 6.1   CONTRADICTORY CONDITIONS FOR BEING AND BECOMING A RESEARCHER

David Boje reflects on these current conditions, which he thinks undermine the possibility of making research an ontological, or even existential stand: 'Most doctoral students don't have the time to become ontological. They got a window where they got a job. And they go in these categories: organizational behaviour, human resources, strategy, operations research. And they have to fit into these boxes to get a job and when they are on the job they have to publish right away – so many articles in six years to get tenure. The clock that they are under doesn't allow for much ontology.'

We believe, as researchers of both today and tomorrow, that it is key to find a balance between academia as a workplace, that is, a special setting with certain requirements and standards that need to be addressed and fulfilled, and academia as a place to play with your own preoccupation with a specific subject, a societal challenge, methodological considerations and/or existential matters – a playground that we believe academia still offers.

WRAPPING UP

Based on the interviews, and in line with Kenneth Gergen, we see theorizing as an *open space*; a room you and others invite and are invited into in order to think, share thoughts and participate in further theory development. Thus, building on the views that have been presented in the previous chapters, the assumption here is that no single published text can contain all there is to say about a topic. There is always room for improvement, extension, criticism and so forth. As such, it is not the individual text that is the contribution. Instead, it is the interest it sparks, the thoughts it gives rise to, and the motivation it creates in others to pick up the ideas and move the thinking forward. Thus, by knowing and reflecting upon how the same research topic can be studied and discussed from different angles and by paying attention to what you prefer, what calls for you to think, and what you are skilled at, it will perhaps become easier to find your own way and voice as a researcher.

As the contributors pinpoint, playing the academic instrument is about resonance. It is about having more than one string to your bow, being able to strike a key, have a good ear for what bounces back and having the patience to restring and restrike again and again. And finally obtaining the professional skills to improvise – to theorize. Hopefully this book has given inspiration to do so.

Appendix: interview question guide – academic theorizing

Contributor:	
Interviewer and date:	
Note taker:	

Introduction
Briefly on the project.
Our own motivation.
On the situation.

1. THE PERSONAL NARRATIVE

What was your background for entering academia?

What influenced your decision to have an academic career?

Thinking back, what have been/are the most thrilling things about being in academia?

2. INSPIRATION

Under what circumstances do you feel most inspired?

Do you deliberately seek inspiration? Where? How?

Can you pinpoint a text (can be everything from a novel, an article, lyrics, poetry etc.) that has been especially inspirational to you?

Have there been different inspirational texts at different points in your life/career?

What texts/articles do you perceive as the canonical texts of your field?

Which role have they played for you (as thought-provoking, inspiration, used to legitimize own writing)?

Can you reflect upon how a text becomes a canon text?

3. THEORIZING

We apply the term to *theorize* – is this meaningful to you (which term would you prefer)? Or what do you understand by theory?

How would you characterize your process of theorizing/theory building (structured/unstructured, creative/analytical)?

What/who supports your thinking?

What can be a barrier to your thinking process?

Looking at your own work, what are the relations between theorizing and the analytical concepts that you have developed?

Personalized section adapted based on the concepts/theories of each contributor:

How did the focus on xxx come about? And how is it related to your application of xxx?

How did the xxx emerge?

How do you perceive your own work; as a model, a theory, an analytical framework or …?

How did you approach existing literature within your field? And which role did the existing literature play with regard to the formulation of the concept of sensemaking (inspiration, criticism of the existing literature, positioning)?

What are you most proud of in your work?

4.   ACADEMIC CRAFTSMANSHIP

We refer to you as a 'giant of organizational research'. This is based on the sentence 'to stand on the shoulders of giants' – what do you perceive by this?

Being a junior researcher how did you approach existing giants?

What would your advice be to present junior researchers?

Does the idea of a giant make it difficult to challenge theory?

In general, there is a focus on identifying knowledge gaps in literature so we can come up with *new* knowledge – what do you think of this 'newness' expectation?

Outro

References

Alford, John (2008), 'The limits to traditional public administration, or rescuing public value from misrepresentation', *The Australian Journal of Public Administration*, **67**(3), 357–66.

Bachelard, Gaston (1958 [2014]), *The Poetics of Space*, London: Penguin Classics.

Bakhtin, Mikhail (1981), *The Dialogic Imagination: Four Essays*, ed. Michael Holquist, Austin, TX: University of Texas Press.

Bartlett, Frederic C. (1932), *Remembering: A Study in Experimental and Social Psychology*, New York: Cambridge University Press.

Boell, Sebastian K. and Dubravka Cecez-Kecmanovic (2010), 'Literature reviews and the hermeneutic circle', *Australian Academic & Research Libraries*, **41**(2), 129–44.

Bourriaud, Nicolas (2002), *Postproduction: Culture as Screenplay: How Art Reprograms the World*, New York: Lukas & Sternberg.

Bunnag, Annawat (2017), 'The concept of time in philosophy: a comparative study between Theravada Buddhist and Henri Bergson's concept of time from Thai philosophers' perspectives', *Kasetsart Journal of Social Sciences*, accessed 16 January 2019 at http://dx.doi.org/10.1016/j.kjss.2017.07.007.

Csikszentmihalyi, Mihaly (1991), *Flow and the Psychology of Discovery and Invention*, New York: Harper Perennial.

Czarniawska, Barbara (2004), 'On time, space, and action nets', *Organization Articles*, **11**(6), 773–91.

Czarniawska, Barbara (2011), 'These shoulders so elegant', in Tommy Jensen and Timothy L. Wilson (eds), *On the Shoulders of Giants*, Lund: Studentlitteratur, pp. 217–32.

De Saussure, Ferdinand (1916 [2011]), *Course in General Linguistics*, New York: Columbia University Press.

Dreyfus, Stuart E. and Hubert L. Dreyfus (1980), *A Five-stage Model of the Mental Activities Involved In Directed Skill Acquisition*, Berkeley, CA: Operations Research Center, University of California, Berkeley.

Edwards, Jeffrey R. and John W. Berry (2010), 'The presence of something or the absence of nothing: increasing theoretical precision in management research', *Organizational Research Methods*, **13**(4), 668–89.

Elbow, Peter (1998), *Writing with Power: Techniques for Mastering the Writing Process*, Oxford: Oxford University Press.

Elsbach, Kimberly, Robert Sutton and David Whetten (eds) (1999), 'Special topic forum on theory development: evaluation, reflections, and new directions', *Academy of Management Review*, **24**(4), 627–806.

Felski, Rita (2008), *Uses of Literature* (Blackwell Manifestos Vol. 71), Malden, MA: Blackwell.

Frankl, Viktor E. (1963), *Man's Search for Meaning*, Boston, MA: Beacon Press.

Gadamer, Hans-Georg (1975 [2013]), *Truth and Method*, London: Bloomsbury Academic.

Genette, Gérard (1997), *Paratexts: Thresholds of Interpretation* (Vol. 20), Cambridge, UK: Cambridge University Press.

Gergen, Kenneth (1991), *The Saturated Self*, New York: Basic Books.

Gladwell, Malcolm (2008), *Outliers: The Story of Success*, London: Hachette UK.

Grant, Maria J. and Andrew Booth (2009), 'A typology of reviews: an analysis of 14 review types and associated methodologies', *Health Information and Libraries Journal*, **26**(2), 91–108.

Guba, Egon G. and Yvonna S. Lincoln (1982), 'Epistemological and methodological bases of naturalistic inquiry', *Educational Communication and Technology*, **30**(4), 233–52.

Hartnack, Justus and Johannes Sløk (eds) (1996), *De store tænkere – Descartes* (*The Great Thinkers – Descartes*), Copenhagen: Munksgaard.

Heidegger, Martin (1927 [2010]), *Being and Time*, Albany, NY: State University of New York Press.

Heidegger, Martin (1968 [2004]), *What is Called Thinking?*, New York: Harper Perennial.

Hernes, Tor (2014), *A Process Theory of Organization*, Oxford: Oxford University Press.

Hobsbawm, Eric J. (1994), *The Age of Extremes: A History of the World, 1914–1991*, New York: Vintage Books.

Hodgkinson, Gerard P. and Denise M. Rousseau (2009), 'Bridging the rigour–relevance gap in management research: it's already happening!', *Journal of Management Studies*, **46**(3), 534–46.

Hofstede, Geert (1983), *Culture's Consequences: International Differences in Work-related Values*, Beverly Hills, CA: Sage.

Holquist, Michael (2003), *Dialogism: Bakhtin and His World*, London: Routledge.

Hustvedt, Siri (2016), *A Woman Looking at Men Looking at Women: Essays on Art, Sex, and the Mind*, London: Simon & Schuster.

Jaccard, James and Jacob Jacoby (2009), *Theory Construction and Model-building Skills: A Practical Guide for Social Scientists*, New York and London: Guilford Press.

Jackson, Patrick T. (2010), 'What is theory?', in Robert A. Denemark (ed.), *The International Studies Encyclopedia*, Blackwell, DOI: 10.1111/b.9781444336597.2010.

Jesson, Jill K., Lydia Matheson and Fiona M. Lacey (2011), *Doing Your Literature Review: Traditional and Systematic Reviews*, Los Angeles, CA: SAGE.

Kieser, Alfred and Lars Leiner (2009), 'Why the rigour–relevance gap in management research is unbridgeable', *Journal of Management Studies*, **46**(3), 516–33.

Koestler, Arthur (1964), *The Act of Creation*, London: Hutchinson.

Kristeva, Julia (1980), *Desire in Language: A Semiotic Approach to Literature and Art*, New York: Columbia University Press.

Kuhn, Thomas S. (1962), *The Structure of Scientific Revolutions*, Chicago, IL: University of Chicago Press.

Lakoff, George and Mark Johnson (1980), *Metaphors We Live By*, Chicago, IL: University of Chicago Press.

Lave, Charles and James March (1975), *An Introduction to Models in the Social Sciences*, New York: Harper & Row.

Liberati, Alessandro, Douglas G. Altman and Jennifer Tetzlaff et al. (2009), 'The PRISMA statement for reporting systematic reviews and meta-analyses of studies that evaluate health care interventions: explanation and elaboration', *PLoS Med*, **6**(7), e1000100, DOI:10.1371/journal.pmed.1000100.

Mac, Anita and Sabine Madsen (eds) (2017), *Forandringsforståelse: balance mellem proces og resultat* (*Understanding Change – The Balance Between Process and Results*), Copenhagen: Samfundslitteratur.

March, James G. (2013), 'In praise of beauty', *M@n@gement*, **5**(16), 732–8.

March, James G. and Herbert A. Simon (1958), *Organizations*, New York: John Wiley & Sons.

McGregor, Douglas (1960 [2006], *The Human Side of Enterprise*, New York: McGraw Hill.

Merton, Robert K. (1965 [1985]), *On the Shoulders of Giants: A Shandean Postscript*, Chicago, IL: University of Chicago Press.

Mintzberg, Henry (2005), 'Developing theory about the development of theory', in Ken G. Smith and Michael A. Hitt (eds), *Great Minds in Management: The Process of Theory Development*, Oxford: Oxford University Press, pp. 355–72.

Mitroff, Ian I. and Ralph H. Kilmann (1978), *Methodological Approaches to Social Science*, San Francisco, CA: Jossey-Bass.

Morgan, David L. (2014), 'Pragmatism as a paradigm for social research', *Qualitative Inquiry*, **20**(8), 1045–53.

Morgan, Gareth (1997), *Images of Organization*, Thousand Oaks, CA: SAGE.

Parini, Jay (2008), *Why Poetry Matters*, Yale, CT: Yale University Press.

Rendtorff, Jacob D. (2014), 'Fænomenologien og dens betydning' ('Phenomenology and its importance'), in Lars Fuglsang, Poul Bitsch Olsen and Klaus Rasborg (eds), *Videnskabsteori i Samfundsvidenskaberne: På tværs af fagkulturer og paradigmer*, Frederiksberg: Samfundslitteratur, pp. 259–88.

Runkel, Philip J. and Margaret Runkel (1984), *A Guide to Usage for Writers and Students in the Social Sciences*, Lanham, MD: Rowman & Littlefield.

Schein, Edgar H. (1956), 'The Chinese indoctrination program for prisoners of war: a study of attempted "brainwashing"', *Psychiatry: Interpersonal and Biological Processes*, **19**(2), 149–72.

Schein, Edgar H. (1969), *Process Consultation: Its Role in Organization Development*, Reading, MA: Addison-Wesley.

Schein, Edgar H. (1985), *Organizational Culture and Leadership*, San Francisco, CA: Jossey-Bass.

Schein, Edgar H. (1999), *Process Consultation Revisited: Building the Helping Relationship*, Reading, MA: Addison-Wesley.

Selye, Hans (1956), *The Stress of Life*, New York: McGraw-Hill.

Stinchcombe, Arthur (1968), *Constructing Social Theories*, Chicago, IL: University of Chicago Press.

Sutton, Robert and Barry Staw (1995), 'What theory is', *Administrative Science Quarterly*, **40**(3), 371–84.

Swedberg, Richard (2012), 'Theorizing in sociology and social science: Turning to the context of discovery', *Theory and Society*, **41**(1), 1–40.

Swedberg, Richard (2014a), *The Art of Social Theory*, Princeton, NJ: Princeton University Press.

Swedberg, Richard (ed.) (2014b), *Theorizing in Social Science: The Context of Discovery*, Stanford, CA: Stanford University Press.

Swedberg, Richard (2016), 'Can you visualize theory? On the use of visual thinking in theory pictures, theorizing diagrams, and visual sketches', *Sociological Theory*, **34**(3), 250–75.

Turner, Stephen (2014), 'Mundane theorizing, bricolage and bildung', in Richard Swedberg (ed.), *Theorizing in Social Science: The Context of Discovery*, Stanford, CA: Stanford University Press, pp. 131–57.

Van der Ven, Andrew (2007), *Engaged Scholarship: A Guide for Organizational and Social Research*, New York: Oxford University Press.

Van de Ven, Andrew and Marshall S. Poole (2005), 'Alternative approaches for studying organizational change', *Organization Studies*, **26**(9), 1377, DOI: 10.1177/0170840605056907.

Webster, Jane and Richard T. Watson (2002), 'Analyzing the past to prepare for the future: writing a literature review', *MIS Quarterly*, **26**(2), 13–23.

Weick, Karl E. (1969), *The Social Psychology of Organizing*, 1st edition, New York: McGraw Hill.

Weick, Karl E. (1979), *The Social Psychology of Organizing*, 2nd edition, New York: McGraw Hill.

Weick, Karl E. (1989), 'Theory construction as disciplined imagination', *Academy of Management Review*, **14**(5), 16–31.

Weick, Karl E. (1995a), 'What theory is not, theorizing is', *Administrative Science Quarterly*, **40**(3), 385–90.

Weick, Karl E. (1995b), *Sensemaking in Organizations*, Thousand Oaks, CA: SAGE.

Weick, Karl E. (2001), *Making Sense of the Organization*, Oxford: Blackwell.

Weick, Karl E. (2005), 'The experience of theorizing: sensemaking as resource and topic', in Ken Smith and Michael Hitt (eds), *Great Minds in Management*, Oxford: Oxford University Press, pp. 394–413.

Weick, Karl E. (2011), 'Organizing for transient reliability: The production of dynamic non-events', *Journal of Contingencies and Crisis Management*, **19**(1), 21–7.

Weick, Karl E. (2014), 'The work of theorizing', in Richard Swedberg (ed.), *Theorizing in Social Science: The Context of Discovery*, Stanford, CA: Stanford University Press, pp. 177–94.

Weick, Karl E. and David P. Gilfillan (1971), 'Fate of arbitrary traditions in a laboratory microculture', *Journal of Personality and Social Psychology*, **17**(2), 179–91.

Weick, Karl E. and Kathleen M. Sutcliffe (2001), *Managing the Unexpected: Resilient Performance*, New York: John Wiley & Sons.

Weick, Karl E. and Kathleen M. Sutcliffe (2007), *Managing the Unexpected: Resilient Performance*, 2nd edition, New York: John Wiley & Sons.

Weick, Karl E. and Kathleen M. Sutcliffe (2015), *Managing the Unexpected: Resilient Performance*, 3rd edition, New York: John Wiley & Sons.

Whetten, David A. (ed.) (1989a), 'Special topic forum on theory development', *Academy of Management Review*, **14**(4), 486–594.

Whetten, David A. (1989b), 'What constitutes a theoretical contribution?', *Academy of Management Review*, **14**(4), 490–95.

Zhao, Shanyang (1996), 'The beginning of the end or the end of the beginning? The theory construction movement revisited', *Sociological Forum*, **11**(2), 305–18.

Index

Printed and bound by CPI Group (UK) Ltd, Croydon, CR0 4YY

09/06/2025

14685770-0001